THE SA
PAINFUL JOURNEY
OF A
Struggling
DISABLED
BLACK MAN

Surviving against all odds. "DON'T QUIT"

CHIBIKE IFECHINELO NWABUDE

outskirtspress
DENVER, COLORADO

Outskirts Press, Inc.
http://www.outskirtspress.com

ISBN: 978-1-4787-5219-6

Outskirts Press and the "OP" logo are trademarks belonging to Outskirts Press, Inc.

PRINTED IN THE UNITED STATES OF AMERICA

Table of Contents

Introduction

I wrote this memoir so that people could understand how frustrated my life had been on this earth. I tried my best to overcome those obstacles and frustrations, but one setback after another, and more setbacks and rejections, just for being a smart disabled black man, dogged me wherever I went.

People should realize that as we strive for a better living, and for a better world, that we need each other's talents, cultures and other attributes of our lives, for a better society, and for the survival of one another. Most importantly, we should try to treat each other just how we should like to be treated, and with compassion.

Disclaimer

This book is based on the true story and some actual events of my life. However, some of the names used, identifying detail and companies described, have been changed to protect the privacy of the individuals and businesses. Any resemblance to the companies, real person, living or dead, is purely coincidental, and unintentional.

My childhood

How I became a disabled person

I was a healthy, normal baby just like every other baby who could walk, run and jump. I did everything that other babies do at that earlier age, but at the age of four, my life took a devastated turn for the worst, and I became a disabled person due to polio illness. The illness that later caused my paralysis, started in one joyous trip my parents took to the village during one of the Christmas celebrations.

I came from a middle class family. My father was a Railroad engineer and my mother owned a Clothing store. My parents were very religious and hard working. They belonged to different organizations in the Catholic Church and they do observe and celebrate Easter and Christmas holidays, and any other traditional festivals that their religious faith embraced. Sometimes, when they took their vacations, they liked to go to the village and be acquainted with other family members.

The Christmas holiday was one of those special functions, when some families arrange for a reunion get together, so that they would socialize and familiarize themselves with the relatives of their families. During those festival occasions, which were organized in the villages, many families travel from different cities of the country to the villages for the reunions. The festivals last for a couple of days, and there were lots of meetings, parties and activities for different age groups to attend.

Since the villages were in a festive mood, many people would gather in the village squares to watch many groups of dancers that dressed in different costumes, while others watch some of the masquerades that whipped themselves to find out who scored the most admiration. These masquerades were very scary looking, because they cover their faces with some witchcraft looking masks, so no one could tell who was underneath those masks. Some of the masquerades visited some peoples in their houses to ask for gifts and money. Sometimes they visited some peoples just to torment them.

It happened that during one of those Christmas festivity gatherings and celebrations, back home in the village, my parents were on vacation and they took the whole family and traveled to the village to spend some time with other family members and relatives. One day my mother left me with a babysitter and went to a social event. Some of those masquerades visited our house, and my baby sister was so frightened and terrified of been whipped by those masquerades, that she abandoned me and ran for her dear life. If she was that terrified, then imagine how terrified a four year old child was at that point, knowing fully well that those masquerades looked like evil spirits. I cried for help, but there was no one to hold and console me. I was so frightened that a few days later, I had a convulsion coupled with high fever, and was taken to the hospital.

At the hospital, one of the medical doctors we saw gave us his diagnoses. He determined that I had a high fever, and he recommended that he would give me some of the medication through an injection.

When he was about to give me the injection on the right side of my thigh, my mother asked him if that was the best area to give me that injection? She told the doctor that she thought that the butt, which have more tissues and could take the length of the needle, was the best area to give me the injection. The Doctor told my mother that he knew better than her where to inject the needle in my body.

He gave my mother the option of taking me home without the medication, or allowing him to inject me where he had already indicated. My mother wanted to ensure that I received some treatment and be cured, so she kept quiet and the doctor gave me the injection where he so desired, and that was on the right side of my thigh. He was supposed to cure my illness, but instead he made it worse. That needle must have hit the bone on my right thigh or any of the nervous system arteries, because it seems that the fluid from the injection ended up going into those areas of my body.

As the high fever subsided, I felt much better, but I gradually became paralyzed. I used to sit, stand, jump and run before I received the high fever medication, but this time, I could not do any of those things any more. Since I could not sit down any more, I lied down on my side and stomach most of the time. I crawled just to move from one place to another, and because of the crawling, some parts of my body were full of blisters and sores. The only time I would sit upright, was when I was fed some foods, or when my mother carried me on her back for a stroll.

A few days later, my mother took me to the hospital and we saw a different doctor. After the diagnosis, she was told that I had polio. From that day forward, I lost the strength and control to some parts of my body, especially in my right leg where I was given the high fever injection medication. My parents suffered a great deal in trying to raise me, now that I was partially paralyzed at that young age. Since I could not sit down, my mother carried me on her lap if I was not lying down on the floor, or she had me on her back most of the time if I was not in the bed.

As a Railroad engineer, my father worked very hard in order to provide the kind of livelihood he wanted for the family. He travelled from one city to another, and sometimes he did not come home for couple of days. My mother took it upon herself and did everything humanly possible to find out if I could be able to regain some strength on some parts of my body, and be able to walk again. For that reason, she took me across the country to some of the orthopedic hospitals where there was any likelihood that I would get some quality treatment. Some other times, she took me to some religious events, where she thought I would be cured miraculously.

My mother carried me most of the time on her back to the hospitals for some of the days I had therapy treatments. Those treatments sometimes last for a few hours of the day, and some rays of high powered beam warmed up the nerves in my legs. The purpose was to revive some of the nerves that were partially weakened by polio, and try to find out, if I would regain some of the strength and functions on those parts of my body.

Since I had the polio at an early age of my life, I missed my childhood. I could not sit down, stand up or run. I was unable to play with other children and was so frustrated. As a child, my parents knew that playing with other children was very important, because it would give me the chance to socialize and associate with them and make me to feel wanted. However, I did not enjoy most of those playing activities some of the times, because some parts of my body hurt.

After many therapy treatments, I was able to sit down, but still could not stand up. Imagine playing with other children, some of them would make fun of me, while few of them would beat me up and ran away. Since I could not run, I sat there and cried. However, if they hit me and stayed there, I would make sure that I beat the hell out of them.

Due to the relentless effort of my parents to insure that I walk again, and with the help of God, I stood up one day to their astonishment, but fell down again. I kept doing that with the assistance of holding on to the chair, table or anything around me for support before I stood up. After so many falls, I was able to stand up, but with the support of an object around me. Then, with the special leg brace I wore in those days, I started getting some strength back on my legs. The doctor instructed me to wear the leg brace most of the time, even while sleeping, to allow for a better blood flow through the veins. Sleeping with the leg brace at night hurts the most, because it was very uncomfortable, and sometimes I would cry almost all through the night for my mother to take it off my leg, so that I would sleep.

Wearing the leg brace could only allow me to sleep on my back, and it was very uncomfortable. My parents were so sympathetic and have seen how uncomfortable it was for me, but because they wanted the best for me and would like to see me walk again, there was nothing they could do, but to have me wear it at night while sleeping just to keep with the doctor's instructions. Sometimes, my crying would get to my mother, because I could see some tears in her eyes. However, with my mother's love for me, she would try to minimize the pains by taking the leg brace off my leg for sometimes, and then put them back on again, so that I could sleep. I was very grateful with all the efforts and the determination of my parents to see me walk again.

Sometimes when I had an appointment with some of the specialist doctors in another city, which was about one hundred and fifty miles away from the city where we lived, my father who was a Railroad engineer, took me to my appointment on a locomotive train. Since he was the Railroad engineer of that train, he would leave me at the passenger section of the train and asked some of his coworkers to take care of me while he drives the train. Along some of the train stops to our destination, he would drop by to know how I was doing before he takes off again.

One of the duties of a Railroad engineer was to drive the train from one city to another, when they were scheduled to work. When they arrived at their destination, they stayed a day or two in guest rest houses or hotels, reserved for them. Then when there was another train going back to their city, they drove that train back to their city.

After visiting the doctors, my father drove the train back home with me in the passenger section. Sometimes, he lets me sit in the locomotive section and I saw how he operated the different control buttons that moved the train. In fact, I was really a burden to my parents, but God gave them the will power and strength to tolerate my severe disability.

My parents spent lots of money on medical bills, and with some hardship, they were able to buy better long leg brace for me, which I wore to sleep without much pain, coupled with other medical equipments they bought for me that helped me walk. After many sleepless nights and with many difficulties, I was able to stand up and walk with the aid of the leg braces. I could attribute my walking today to the relentless efforts of my parents. I later outgrew those leg braces and did not wear them for a long period in my life.

During those periods when I did not wear the leg brace on my right leg, I used my right hand to support the leg while walking. That was because the right knee was very weak and I had to support it in order to move my left leg. The only disadvantage was that any time my hand got tired, and I did not support my right leg with enough strength, I fell down. I had fallen too many times, that the only way to avoid the frequent fall was to make and wear another leg brace. Now I wear a very nice and comfortable long leg brace on my right leg. I only wear it if I am going outside of the house, because it helps to support my balance while walking and prevent me from falling down. Once I get home, I take it off, because I could walk inside the house without the leg brace.

My babysitter and me

In the city of Zaria where we lived, my mother had a small clothing store where she made and sold clothing. She also trained some people on how to make and sew women's clothing. Some of her student workers paid her a certain amount of money to learn the trade on how to make and sew women's clothing.

Due to the hectic work schedule of my father, he sometimes stayed out of our home for a few days. My mother was so busy running her business, and sometimes her students would need her attention so much that she did not have much time to spend with the family. Therefore, my parents decided that they would get a babysitter that would live with us, take care of the children, and help with some other chores in the house. They contacted some of our relatives for recommendations on who to hire for the babysitter job.

Some family members recommended some of the daughters of their neighbors, while some recommended other female relatives for the job. After few weeks of searching, my parents hired a babysitter from a family friend of one of our relatives. They paid her transportation to travel from the eastern part of the country to Zaria, which was in the northern part of the country, and it took about two days journey by train. At the time this babysitter came to live with us, she was about eighteen years old and I was about seven years old.

She was so innocent looking and very hard working for the first year she lived with us. She took care of my siblings and me very well, that my mother trusted her with many things in our house, and she knew where my mother kept her money in our house. She kept the house clean, helped with the cooking, and fed me and my younger brothers and sister.

My mother had a lot of confidence in the babysitter to take care of us and the house, that sometimes, she left the house for many hours, running her business and seeing some clients, with no worries that my siblings and I are in good hands at home. In fact, my mother sometimes thanked the people that recommended the babysitter to our family.

After the babysitter stayed with us for about one year, she started to have special affection for me, may be because of my disability. She paid more attention to me more than she did for my younger brothers and sister. At that time, she was nineteen years old and I was eight years old.

The caring and innocent looking babysitter that everybody liked in my family, turned out to be one of the nightmares from hell that any child would never dream to have. The affection that this babysitter had for me gradually developed into sexual feelings for me. She started by touching my penis whenever she dressed me up after given me a bath. Any time she touched my penis, I had an erection. Though it felt strange to me at that age to see that part of my body got so hard and erected whenever she touched me there, but I did not know what it was used for, and why it was so erected.

Once she saw that I would get an erection any time she touched my penis, she then took it a step further. This time she wanted to have sex with me, and one of the ways to accomplish that was to have sex with me in the bathroom. She knew that if she tried having sex with me in any part of our house, that she would be caught, because we lived in a three bedroom apartment at the time.

The sexual molestation started when I was eight years old and went on for about five years until I was thirteen years old. Most of the sexual abuse happened in the bathroom when she took me with her to take some shower. The kind of bathroom we had in most of the cities in Nigeria at that time, did not have water running out from the showerhead. When someone wanted to take a shower, he or she had to fill the bucket with hot and cold water, carry it into the bathroom and then take a shower. She used my disability as an excuse to sexually abuse me, because she stated that I would not be able to give myself a bath.

Sometimes she would take me and my younger brothers and sister to the bathroom and gave us some bath. However, she always made sure that she gave them bath first, and then had each of them leave the bathroom. Then I was the last one left with her. Just because she took care of me, and was very protective of me, my parents trusted her. They never suspected that I was sexually molested, even when they were at home. It never occurred to them that someone they trusted would sexually abuse me.

It was inconceivable that my parents were at home when most of the sexual molestation took place, and they never knew that I was sexually abused. The reason was that, when the babysitter wanted to take her own shower, she would take me with her, and that eliminated any suspicion that I was having sex with her. Most of the sex I had with her was doggy style kind of sex, since we were in the bathroom.

During those incidents, I knew that I had an erection and felt the sensation of ejaculation, but did not ejaculate anything from my penis. I also felt the sensation of ejaculation when she touched my penis, gave me oral sex, and when she bend over and asked me to have sex with her from behind, since we are in the bathroom. After I had sex with her for a while, I was very curious at that age and wanted to know how babies were born. So when I learnt that babies were born by having sexual intercourse, I became scared that I might have a child, even though I was still a child myself.

I recalled one day, I asked my mother too many questions about sex and how babies were born. She stopped me, and asked me why I was asking that many questions about sex. I told her that I was just curious to know. However, what she did not know was that I was terrified and hiding in fear about what the babysitter told me. She told me that she would kill me, if I ever told anyone that we were having sex.

Sometimes when my parents went to visit some friends and I was at home with the babysitter, we had sex. Imagine how fearful I was to think at that age that I might have gotten her pregnant, though I never ejaculated during the sexual act with her.

How could I say no to her when she was in control of me, and with the kind of threat she had over me, I obliged to her sexual demands. Sometimes when my parents wanted to go visit some family friends, I volunteered to go with them just to avoid not being alone with the babysitter, because I knew that any time we were alone and nobody was around, she always had sex with me. There were sometimes when my parents wanted me to go out with them, but the babysitter would give them an excuse for me to stay home with her and they would oblige. Once they left, she would wait for a few minutes just to make sure they were not coming back into the house, and then we had sex.

One day I overheard my parents discussed that we might travel home to the village during one of the Christmas holidays. I was very happy, because I knew that the babysitter would not be able to have sex with me if we travel to the village, due to the fact that the atmospheres in the village were totally different from what we had in the city. The bathrooms, we had in the villages were not built with bricks, and someone could pretty much see the head of the person taken a shower, if they walk closer to the bathrooms, because the walls were built with palm trees leaves.

Though my parents had decided that we would travel to the village for Christmas, but they did not set the date of the travel. I must have asked them for the actual date of the travel many times, that they thought that I must have had a change of mind about the village life, and began to like it. My parents knew that I hated going to the village, because of the poor sanitation there. If the city life in Nigeria was not conducive for a disabled person, imagine how the village life would be. In those days in the village, there were no electricity, no tap water, the roads were not tarred, and most of them were not drivable.

Some people that own cars would walk some blocks from where they parked their cars to their houses, because the roads were narrow pathways used for walking only. Some families do not have toilet facilities in their homes, and they had to go into the bushes to defecate. I hated village life for all those reasons and more. However, here I was, asking my parents for the date we were to travel to the village for holidays.

My parents could not believe it, because like I said before, they knew that I hated going to the village, so for me to be too happy that we were going to the village for the holidays, was so strange to them, but they went ahead with the plan. They did not know that all I wanted to do was to get away from the babysitter from hell, who had been abusing me sexually for many years. If they knew the mental anguish the babysitter had put me through, they would have sent her packing and moved her out from our house.

When my parents finally chose the date of the travel, I was very happy and I looked forward to the date. It happened that the Christmas holiday which my parents chose for us to travel to the village, was during one of the Christmas holidays the village people had chosen as general home coming reunion for the whole town people. My father booked our reservation on a first class coach with the Railways, three weeks in advance. We were very excited and looked forward for the journey, because to travel by Train from the northern part of the country where we lived to the eastern part of the country takes about two days. In the first class coach, we had all the necessary amenities needed as if someone rented a one bedroom from a hotel. I was still having sex with the babysitter just before we traveled.

The day we travelled, we enjoyed the restaurant foods on the Train, saw the beautiful sceneries of the coastal towns and villages. The Railways have some stations where Trains could stop for longer minutes for the Railroad engineers to change shifts. In those stations, people on the Train were allowed to leave the Train, go to some nearby shops and buy some items or do some sightseeing. When the Train was about to leave the station, it blows its horns to signal that it was about to leave, and whoever was in the Train before it stopped, knew it was time to get back into the Train for the next destination. The Train gradually left the station at five miles per hour and then picks up speed once that station was behind us. When we got to our destination, we left the Train station, and went to the taxi parks where we caught the vehicles that took us from that city to the village, which was about an hour drive.

When we arrived at the village, it was very difficult to have sex with my babysitter, because the bathroom walls were built with the leaves of palm trees. Depending on how the bathroom was built, people walking around could see either the legs or the head of someone taken a shower, if that person is tall enough. Therefore, it was not conducive for sex. The villages had busy atmosphere, because some people who had not seen my family for a long time and heard that we were home, came by to say hello. There were no quiet places for the babysitter to have sex with me without been seen.

I noticed that the babysitter was spending lots of time with one of my uncles. She traveled with him to other villages, and sometimes they spent the night together. The month we spent in the village was one of the best months of my life, because I did not have sex with my babysitter.

When it was time for me and my parents to go back to the city, so that my father would resume his work, my uncle told my parents that he wanted to marry the babysitter, and as such, she would not go back with us to the city. When I heard that news, only God knew what kind of relief and excitement I had, that she was not going back with us to the city, because my nightmare would be over.

As the date of our departure got closer, all I had been thinking and prayed to God, was for my uncle not to change his mind about mar-rying the babysitter. We lived in the northern part of the country and my father had already booked our travel reservation on the Train that would take us back home. To go to the Train station, we had to travel with a motor truck from the village to the city, and then board the Train that traveled two days before we got home.

On the very day of our departure, we started boarding the motor truck that would take us to the city. I did not believe that the babysitter was not traveling with us, until she came and gave me a hug, and we said the last goodbye to each other. However, after the goodbye, I thought that she might change her mind to travel with us. If that happened, here comes my nightmare all over again.

I sat very quietly in the motor truck with all those molestation thoughts going through my mind, and I waited eagerly for the rest of the people that would travel with us to the city to come aboard. As the last person boarded the vehicle and the door was closed, I could not believe that the babysitter was not traveling with us, until the vehicle slowly drove away from the compound.

I saw that the babysitter was crying and waving goodbye, but I still could not believe my eyes, because I thought it was still possible for someone to shout for the vehicle to stop for her to come in. Deep inside my mind, I was just full of joy and relieved, but I did not want to show my emotions. As the vehicle took a turn, and I lost sight of the babysitter, that was when I breathed a sigh of relief that my nightmare was partially over. On the way to the city, I was full of joy, but refrained from showing it, because she could change her mind about the marriage to my uncle, and would want to travel with us.

When we arrived at the Train station, I was still not sure that my nightmare was over between the babysitter and me. I still thought that she might show up before we boarded the Train to say that she changed her mind, and that she was traveling with us. I maintained my cool, but kept track of the time, because it seems as if the time was not moving fast enough for me until we boarded the Train.

My mother noticed that I was too quiet, and she asked me what was wrong with me. I told her that I was okay. Once the Train started moving away slowly, and it finally left the station, the relief I had in my mind was awesome. I do not know how to describe it, but it was the type of relief, that adds some years to some one's life span. If my parents were vigilant to observe my mood, they would have noticed that I did not miss that the babysitter did not travel with us one bit, because I never asked them any questions about the babysitter.

The day we traveled back to the city without the babysitter was the last time I saw or heard from her. Remember what I said that the babysitter told me, that if I ever told anyone that we had sex, that she would kill me. I never told anybody in my family about the sexual abuse with the babysitter, even when it was obvious that she would never come and live with my family again. I just wanted to move on with my life.

The babysitter finally married my uncle who had two other wives. She had three children with my uncle. When he died, she had four other children with four different men, with no one to take care of the children. My father saw the poor condition of the children and helped them with their problems. So he ended up taking care of some of those children, and gave them the kind of opportunities that each of his own children had. He had some of them lived with us in other to provide them with foods, shelter and paid their school fees.

Some of them stole money and different items from my parents, but my father still gave each of them a chance to prove that they could be productive in life. Our family was very religious, but some of the children did not like to go to church, and those that were in school, did not want to be educated, so they dropped out of school. My father helped each one of the children as much as he could, until they decided that they had enough of my family. They left and lived the kind of lives they wanted with their mother. My father did not interfere with their lives anymore, since he could not force someone to accept some help if they do not want any help.

Being a disabled black man

Being a disabled man had been very difficult emotionally, psychologically and physically. As a disabled person, I was confronted with many discriminatory factors in my life. Just being a disabled person was difficult by its self, but being a disabled black man was a bad combination in my life. Not only do I have to deal with the discrimination of being black, but I also have to deal with the discrimination of being a disabled person. Therefore, I had some obstacles to overcome in life in order to succeed.

Some disabled people were not given the opportunities to prove that they could do many things in life. Take myself as a typical example. I knew that I am talented and intelligent and could do many things if given the opportunity, but that opportunity was far from coming. Not given that opportunity to reach my potential in life, was so frustrating that I could not find a word to describe it. I am a religious person, and sometimes I asked God, was I created in this world only to be witnessing all these atrocities and injustices?

Among the industrialized nations, United States of America have done a lot to accommodate disabled people in the society and in the work force, knowing fully well that no condition in life is permanent. Meaning that, one might be a healthy person today, but due to unforeseen circumstances, things might change in the future, and that same person might end up being a disabled person too.

We still have some people that stereotype some disabled people as not very intelligent. Therefore, if a disabled person wanted to be accepted in whatever endeavors they are doing, they have to prove beyond a reasonable doubt, that they could do that task, and by so doing, a lot of stress is put on that individual.

I am a gifted and talented person, but never had the opportunity to show my talent. Sometimes I felt that if the gift that God had given me was used to its fullest potentials, that everybody around me would have benefited from it. However, for the fact that I was not given that opportunity, just because I am a disabled black person, was quite unfortunate and frustrating.

A peek at my sad struggling life

It appeared as if whatever I wanted to do in life, did not go the way I planned it. There would always be some obstacles and frustrations along the way. My life was full of one disappointment after another, and it never seems to have an end. I am a Christian, and sometimes when I pray, I asked God this question, why me? What have I done in this world to deserve being discriminated against, and looked down upon just because I am a disabled black man?

In my prayer, I asked God to forgive me my sins, and if I had done something wrong to any one, or offended any one directly or indirectly, let God please forgive me, and I promise never to do that again. I always ask God, to give me the strength and will power to overcome all these misfortunes and tribulations. I also pray that with the little possessions God had given me, for him to help me to be generous and kind towards my fellow human beings.

There were many times I had cried myself to sleep. Sometimes while I was driving, tears would drop out of my eyes, because I was crying inside. As I was crying and meditating, I would ask God to forgive me all my sins, and to please better my condition in life, so that I would be able to help many people in need. I have had many sleepless nights thinking, and sometimes I asked myself, what have I done to deserve all these injustices from some people, the discriminations I had at any of the jobs that I had worked, and during my college days?

Some of those discriminations were from different races, particularly at my jobs. The last incident of discrimination I had at my job was with a black American female. I never imagined that I would be discriminated against from someone who was black like me. However, that discrimination turned out to be one of the worst discriminations I have ever had so far in my life. That black woman was very mean, and a bully from hell.

Sometimes in the middle of the night, I woke up and tried to figure out some solutions to my problems, but would not come up with any immediate remedies. Instead, I would end up with lots of headaches. Even with all my problems, I still ask God, that his will be done, and that my prayers be answered at an acceptable time for him. I also ask God to have mercy on me, and lessen my suffering, and most importantly, give me the will power to withstand the suffering and pains. At the same time, I asked God to please continue to use me to do his will.

When I said suffering, I do not mean suffering from my health, though I am already a disabled person, which was an impediment on its own. Apart from that, my health was perfectly okay, with the exception of the leg ulcer treatment I had, which had healed. The suffering I talked about, was the emotional roller coaster that I went through in my life. The injustices and discriminations I had all through my life, with the stress and emotional anguishes associated with it, both at my job and social life, had been too overwhelming.

I do not like injustices, and because of that, I had tried as much as I could to be fair in whatever I did, and tell the truth regardless of the consequences. The way things are going in my life, I do not think that I might die a natural death, because someone might harm me, due to my honesty, since I am an advocate for justice and equality for all humanity.

One thing is certain for sure, I will never kill myself, steal, do illegal activities or be mischievous in order to achieve my goals and minimize my sufferings in life. I cannot stand injustice towards me or to others. I like all races, and I do not discriminate against anyone. I had been discriminated against and belittled, to the point that sometimes I questioned myself, or doubt my own ability to do and achieve certain things in life. After each day had come and gone, I kept telling myself, remember, you had not achieved much in life, at least to the point where I feel I should be able to help other people and be satisfied in life.

I got older each day that passed by, and yet, I had not accomplished the goals I set for myself. For example, getting married and having kids, have enough money, so that I would be able to help others in need, plan for my retirement, and many other things in life that I knew at my age, that I would have been able to accomplish by now. Sometimes I said to myself, maybe I did not do enough in order to break those barriers. But I cannot kill myself in order to achieve my goals in life.

At times, I thought about giving up on life, and not striving any longer. However, another inner thought would say to me, do not give up, because if you do, God might prolong your life on this earth, and then you will live to regret it. I do not like to use this regrettable word "Had I known". Had I known, I would have done this or that? That is the reason why I try as much as possible to be perfect in whatever I do, or at least come closer in making it perfect. I am the kind of person that hurts emotionally when things go wrong, especially if it involves my rationale. I would blame myself so much when things go wrong, that I would say to myself, if I had done it this way or that way, may be it would not have gone wrong in the first place. Therefore, I chose to keep striving in life and hope for the best one day.

Having lived through a lot of injustices and prejudices in my life, I find it difficult to trust anyone. God is the only one I trust, and I beg him to save me from those misfortunes and predicaments. I always ask God, when is the agony in my life going to be over? Please God, do not let my kindness kill me one day. At the same time, let the will of God be done. I also have to thank my parents, my brothers and sisters, because they are the only people I could run to in times of difficulties and expect them to help me, and they had been an inspiration to my survival.

With the emotional roller coaster kind of life I experienced, I composed a poem in those days entitled loneliness, to reflect what happened in my life, how I lived, struggled, and overcame certain obstacles in my life. Any way here is the poem.

Loneliness

Loneliness, loneliness, loneliness, day and night you are there stirring at my face. Knowing how you are, I never wanted you as a friend, nor do I want your association. Any time I want to get away from you, rejection draw me close to you, and then frustration and injustices draw me even closer to you. Loneliness, the question that I keep asking you was this. What have I done wrong in my life that was so outrageous or rather unforgiving that the consequences are that I should be your friend? Why me?

I always try harder to show people that I love them, regardless of their race or national origin. Loneliness, do I not deserve to be loved too? Any time I extended my friendship and love for others, here come rejection, injustices, and before you know it, I am back to you. Stupid loneliness, why do I have those rejections and injustices? I do not like you.

I have always worked harder than most people, just to show that I am talented and intelligent, and I have been begging for opportunities to contribute my talent to the society. Instead, being a disabled black person, became an obstacle in achieving those goals. Then, before you know it, here comes stupid loneliness again welcoming me back.

Loneliness, loneliness, loneliness, you do not come into any one's life unless you are allowed to come into the person's life. I do not even want to know you, let alone allowing you into my life. But your stupid door was always open to welcome people into your stupid world. Repeatedly, I kept running back to you due to racism and injustices that had confronted me in my life. I cried for help, and deep inside my heart, I begged for love and acceptance, but no one seems to hear my grievances, except you, stupid loneliness. I wish I never know you.

Loneliness, loneliness, loneliness, if you know how much I hate you, you should not even try to come into my life. However, it seems that the chains of events keep drawing me closer to you. I like to socialize and make people laugh and happy, but when I encounter injustice, you are always there to welcome me back, even though associating with you always have some sadness in my life.

I am a generous and a lenient person, but injustice and racism never allowed me to prosper, so that I could take care of other people in need. I always sacrifice my own welfare and the last penny I have, trying to help someone in need, and I have gone broke while doing that. But what do I get in return for my generosity? Some people took my kindness as a weakness, while other people took advantage of my kindness, and put me in a jeopardizing position, to the extent that I had been broke helping them.

With all those misfortunes in my life one after another, I came to the conclusion that I prefer to suffer, rather than seeing other people suffer, especially someone that I care the most. I prefer to die rather than seeing the people I love and cared for die before me. When people are suffering and dying and I cannot help them, it tends to depress me, and before you know it, here comes loneliness, begging me to come back home again.

Loneliness, loneliness, Loneliness, you know how to get to me. Because when people take advantage of me when I am trying to do some kindness, my trust in them diminishes, and before you know it, here comes stupid loneliness, knocking at my door and asking if I want to come back home.

Loneliness, I hope you know why I never wanted to be your friend. Any time I am with you, I cry most of the time, I do not have friends to trust or tell my problems, because it is only you and me. Loneliness, if you know how much I wanted to be loved and cherished, and verse versa, you should never ever associate yourself with me.

Loneliness, I have many chances in breaking away from you and associating myself with other people. But when lack of trust, injustice and racism show their ugly heads again, Loneliness, you are there to invite me with open arms and I stupidly run back to you for a painful and sorrowful comfort. Loneliness, loneliness, loneliness, how I wish I never know you.

Loneliness, you know what, after all you have put me through and I have not broken down yet, I think I am now immune to you. I am not scared of you anymore. I do not like you and will never accept you as my friend, because you always want me to come and join you so that we can be lonely together.

Loneliness, you know that I have always wanted to be a priest and live a holy life. So is it because I changed my mind not to be a priest, because of my disability that you wanted to show me how lonely I would be for not chosen to be a priest. That is not right. Though I am not a priest, but every day of my life, I try as much as possible to come closer to my God. Therefore, if you think that being lonely was to teach me a lesson, you are wrong. Because I rather save my soul by doing the will of God, than lose it. I have tried as much as possible not to join you when you invite me, but circumstances tend to bring us together. Remember what I said, that I am so immune to you now, because I did not let you control or destroy me emotionally. Stupid loneliness.

Loneliness, loneliness, loneliness, to be honest with you, sometimes I do not even feel I am with you anymore, because I am so use to you. Thanks to the internet, where I can spend many times doing many of the things that occupied my mind, that I do not even feel I am with you.

Loneliness, I have come to the conclusion or rather a realization that you might be part of my life in as much as I never like you. Deep inside my heart, I am hurting emotionally sometimes, but people around me do not know when I am with you. Loneliness, I wish I never know you. God, I wish I did not have to go through those misfortunes in life that introduced me to Loneliness. However, please God, help me to endure it all with love and patience, for your time is the best, and let your will be done. Loneliness, I wished I never know you.

Nigerian civil war where some of the struggles of my life started

The Nigerian civil war was one of the worst periods of my life that I do not like to discuss, because of the politics about that war. I would only talk about the war, because of how it affected the lives of my family, especially my life, and how it was one of the most depressed parts of my life. The Nigerian civil war was fought for more than three years, and to this day, I could not pinpoint the main reason why that war was fought.

All I would say was that the British government benefited a lot from that war, because they were the colonial master before Nigeria got her independence. Nigeria got her independent from the British Government without shedding any blood for it. When Britain discovered that the newly independent country had many crude oils and other mineral resources, they instigated that war among the people of Nigeria, and then took advantage of it and ripped the country off millions of dollars of crude oil.

My father was a Railroad engineer; and he was transferred from one city to another very often. Sometimes within two years or less, he was transferred twice to different cities. One of the cities where we lived for a long period was Zaria, which was in the northern state of Nigeria. With the amount of money my father earned, he tried as much as possible to give us the best that life could afford. He built a double acre house in that city.

When the house was been built, the whole member of my family sacrificed our time and efforts towards the building of the house. Any day my father was off work, he spent most of his time directing and overseeing the progress of the house. We moved into the house few months after it was finished, and my father was about to buy a car when the Nigerian civil war started in 1967.

My family lived in the northern part of the country, which was mostly occupied by the Muslim Hausas. When the war started, we abandoned everything my parents worked and saved as civil servants behind and ran for our dear lives to Enugu, a city in our hometown in the eastern part of the country where majority of the occupants were the Igbos and mostly Christians.

As the war progressed with no end in sight, the Igbos tried to secede from Nigeria, and the name of the new country was Biafra. Some countries around the world recognized Biafra as an independent country, while others did not. The United State of America did not recognize Biafra as an independent country, and for that reason, there was no moral and military support to sustain the war with Nigerian troops. As the war went on, Nigerian troops kept advancing toward Enugu, which was the capital city of Biafra. During the day and at night, Nigerian airplanes attacked the city, and they bombed both the civilians and military installations.

It was obvious that the Nigerian troops would capture the city of

Enugu, and it was only a matter of time for that to happen. I was a nervous wreck whenever I heard the sound of incoming artillery shells or the sound of bombs been dropped from fighter planes. The reason was that, I knew that when it gets so dangerous for people to run for their lives, that I could not run because of my disability.

We found out every day, that the Nigerian troops had advanced towards Enugu city where we lived. At night when everywhere was so quiet, you would hear the sound of the artillery shells from the Nigerian troops louder, and the sound of bomb explosions dropped from the air raids. We could rarely sleep at night without been awakened by those noises.

Some of the wealthy Igbo people, who were in the business of transportation, had many buses and motor trucks that they used for their businesses. It happened that one of those men had about fifty or more of his vehicles that he wanted to move away from Enugu, before Nigerian troops took over the city where his company was located. So he announced to the public that if anyone could put some gas in any of the vehicles, that they could use that vehicle to transport themselves out of Enugu, and out of the arms way of the advancing Nigerian troops.

The only favor he asked from the people that took his vehicles, was that after they used those vehicles to transport their families wherever they wish, that they returned them to his new company location, which was in the interior of Imo State called Okiewe. One of the brothers of my mother had already taken one of those vehicles and ran to another city in Imo state. It happened that some other relatives from my mother's side of the family were fortunate to have one of those big motor trucks from the company.

My parents knew that I would not be able to run if there was panic and the whole city of Enugu started running, because Nigerian troops were advancing toward the city every day. So they arranged for me to travel with my relatives. My mother told them to take me with them to any city where they ran to, and that if they later found out the city where his brother had ran to with his family, that they would drop me off there.

I traveled with my mother's relatives to one of the refugee camps in one of the cities in another state. We stayed there for about three months, and as Nigerian troops advanced towards that part of the city, we ran again to Okiewe, which was another city farther away into the state. That was where we brought back the vehicle to the company that owned it.

Enugu was the capital of Biafra, and it was captured by Nigerian troops within a few months that Biafra declared her independent. Before the city of Enugu was captured my Nigerian troops, my family ran from there to another city which was in the interior part of the state. Again, they lost all the properties they had in Enugu.

I did not know if my family members made it alive when the city of Enugu was captured, because I did not hear from my parents, and did not know their way about for more than a year. There was no phone communication, no letters since there were no Post Offices. One of the best communication methods people used at that time to hear from some love once was through the drivers that transported goods and services, and people through different refugee camps to deliver some foods.

Any time I saw new refugees that were brought into our camps, I asked some of them and the drivers, if they knew or heard any information about my family or there were about, and if they knew someone who was inquiring about me? Finally, one day, one of the drivers that dropped off some of the refugees, showed one of the refugee the name of a person written on a piece of paper, and asked him if he knew that person? That name happened to be my name, and the refugee told the driver, yes.

He showed the driver where I was staying in the camp, and when the driver met me, he told me that my parents were alive and was inquiring to know the city where I lived. The driver then told me the city where my family lived. That was a joyful moment for me, because I thought they did not make it alive when Nigerian soldiers captured Enugu. Before the driver left, I gave him some personal note with some comments that would convince my parents that the driver saw me.

Living in one of those refugee camps was not easy. Those camps were elementary schools or secondary school buildings converted into refugee camps. Some people, who could afford beds, brought their own beds, while the others slept on mats spread on the floors. There was no privacy, so whatever anyone did, was in the open for the rest of the people to watch.

The toilet facilities did not work since many of the states at that time did not have reliable tap water to support the toilet systems. Therefore, everybody defecated in the bushes around the refugee camps. Diarrheas were the common diseases suffered by many people who lived in those camps, because flies flew from the wasted human feces to the foods eaten by the refugees. Malnutrition was another problem in those camps, because many people did not have balanced diets. People bathed and washed dirty clothes in the stream they fetched for their drinking water, and that stream was about five to seven miles away from the refugee camps.

After I heard that my parents were alive and communicated with them, they told me to go and live with my brother in laws. It took me another eight months before I was reunited and lived with my brother in laws and their families who ran to a different state. They lived in a big compound that was given to them by some friends. The city where we lived was notorious for kidnapping. Some of our goats and sheep were stolen every other day. Then we wondered what else they would steal. My brother in laws decided that instead of waking up one day, and one of us would not be found, that it was time to move out of that city.

The next city where we went and lived was susceptible to the air raids by the Nigerian warplanes. Sometimes they flew by the city during the day and dropped some bombs in the war fronts. I recalled one incident that happened one day when I went to a nearby hospital for treatment. When I was walking home after the treatment, one of the Nigerian warplanes flew very low and was looking for its target. I was so scared that I took cover and dived into nearby bushes. I did not know that the whole bushes were covered with barbed wires. When I dived into the bushes with my belly on the ground, those wires pierced my skin, head and feet, I was covered with blood, and there was nobody around to help me. It took me some time to get out of that mess. When I got out, I swore to God, that next time if there was an air raid, that I would not take cover again. I reached the conclusion that if it was the will of God that I would die during the war, no matter what I did, I would die, if it was not the will of God, then I would not die.

I stayed with my brother in laws for more than one year, before I was reunited with my parents. There were no air raids from Nigerian warplanes in the city where my parents lived in the refugee camps. In fact, my family suffered during the civil war, and my father did all he could to support our family, that he travelled more than one to two hundred miles by bike to buy and sell some foodstuffs, so that we would survive.

During the civil war, some men were conscripted to serve in the army. To avoid conscription into the army, my father grew his white beard, long enough that he looked just like the beard of Santa Clause. The beard made him look much older than his age. That was the reason he was not conscripted to join the army. Any one that saw him would think that he was a ragged homeless old man. When the civil war ended, he shaved off the beard and became his normal self once again.

The mysterious way the Nigerian civil war started, that was how it ended. We woke up one day, looked at the streets, and saw many men walking in all directions along the roads with civilian clothes. We did not hear the sound of the artillery shells, which we normally hear during that time of the day. Words spread that the war was over, and that Biafra troops have surrendered to Nigerian troops. People were scared, and the first thought in every one's mind at that time was that Nigerian troops would start killing people at random, since they have taken over the government, and the name Biafra did not exist anymore.

Then we heard that they were some negotiated arrangements between the Nigeria government and some top officials of the Biafra government before the surrender. One of the arrangement stipulated that anyone who laid down their arms and went home, would be granted an amnesty by the Nigeria government. As the days passed by, fears subsided and the whole people in the refugee camps started to plan on how to go to their different towns and cities, to see what was left of their properties, or destroyed during the civil war.

I could only say that we were lucky to have survived the civil war. It added some more setbacks to any of the goals that I set to achieve in life, bearing in mind that my disability had already set me back many years, by preventing me from going to school at an early age of my life. My family had to gather the little properties we had after the war, and started rebuilding our lives all over again.

I do not want to discuss much about the Nigerian civil war any more, because it was so painful to me. With all the hardship I endured during that war with my disability, I did not know how I survived that war. I wasted three to four years of my life in a stupid war, which to this day I did not know for sure why we fought that war. Nigerian civil war was a painful memory to me, which I do not want to relive in this memoir, and for that reason, I would not talk about it anymore.

The first stage of my education experience

I started school very late in life, because of my disability. My parents realized very early in my life that the only thing that would help me in my life was education. They knew that if I was educated, that I would be able to get a job and support myself. So for that reason, my parents did everything possible by sacrificing their time and welfares in order to take me to school, and sometimes when it was not possible for me to go to school, they hired a teacher to come to our home to teach me and my brothers and sisters Mathematics, English and some other courses.

When I started going to elementary school, it was too late when compared to the age that other average children started going to school. That was due to my disability, but once I started going to school, I loved it, and because my parents wanted me to be educated, they did everything possible to relief the suffering I would have encountered while going to school. Sometimes they would arrange with family friends to drive me to and from school. They tried to live closer to the schools, so when there was no ride, I could walk a short distance to and from school.

My mother arranged for teachers to come to our house on certain days of the week to teach us some study lessons, and guide us on our home works. She would make sure that we did our home works before we go to bed each day. She accomplished that by cooking dinner on time, and then fixed every one's plate. She would then instruct us that whoever finished his or her homework would go and eat dinner. With that in mind, every one of us strived to do our homework on time.

I would attribute my knowledge and love of mathematics to those study lessons I received from the private teachers that came to our house and taught us some courses. I remembered how I asked the teachers many questions whenever I did not understand how we got the solution to some of the mathematics problems. I loved mathematics, because it made me think a lot while I was trying to solve a problem. Also, it was one of the courses that I could understand easily and follow logically. Loving mathematics made me to be analytical and logical in my thinking, and I tried as much as possible to be perfect in whatever I do in my life.

As a disabled person, whenever I am walking, I am always conscious of my walk, because I do not have much balance on the ground when I am walking. I can easily fall down if I trip on something or slip on a wet floor.

The hardship I encountered when I went to elementary school was unbearable and sometimes humiliating, because I did not have any leg brace at that time. I fell down too many times that I lost count of the number of falls. In the many falls that I had, I had broken my hand, bruised my whole body or dislocated my ankle when I accidentally sat on that leg. When it rained and the whole floor was wet, I could easily lose my balance if I slipped and fell. When I fell down on a wet floor, to get up from it was a hassle and without any help from someone, I would just sit there, because to stand up, I had to hold on something in order to get up from the floor.

Most of the buildings in the schools were not accessible for the disabled people. The stairs in the buildings of the classrooms did not have handrails for someone to hold on while climbing the stairs. So to go up those stairs, I had to sit on the stairs, and then use my two hands to climb the stairs one at a time until I get to the top level, then I hold on something to get up and walk.

Sometimes when I got to the top level of the stairs, I had to sit and rest to catch my breath before I stood up and walk again. When I got up, my hands and my pants were dirty with dusts. Imagine doing the same thing whenever it rained and the stairs were all muddy from the soles of the students' shoes that used the stairs. Anyway, I knew that with education I would have a brighter future, so I preserved through all those stresses, just to be educated.

In school, I did not indulge in rough sports or played any kind of sports were pushing and standing up was involved. I enjoy board games better, because I could sit down while I played the games. When I played with some of the students, some of the malicious once knew that I could not run, so when they were mad at me, they would push me down and ran away. I just sat there, cried and grieved. However, if they did not run away when they pushed me down, and decided to confront me, I would beat the hell out of them. Those incidents happened in elementary school, because I did not have that much problem with the students in high school, since I picked my own friends. I also tried to avoid any trouble as much as possible.

I recalled one day in high school, we were in the classroom and I told an expensive joke about one of my classmate. This student stood up, approached my desk, and then slapped me so hard that all of his five fingers made a scar on my face. One thought inside of me told me to retaliate, and another thought said to me, do not retaliate, because if

I did not made that joke about him, I would not have been slapped. Therefore, I decided not to retaliate. I just turned around, sat down and started doing my class work as if the slap did not hurt. But it hurt so much that I was lost for word, because I did not know what to say to the student that slapped me.

Since I did not retaliate or said a word to him, he did not know what I had in mind, and to be honest with you, I did not have anything in mind, because without the expensive joke I made, I would not have been slapped. A few days later, this student came and apologized for what he did to me and both of us became friends again. I am the kind of a person that tries to avoid confrontations with people at all cost, but if the situation happened, and I was caught up in it, I would evaluate the situation and then solve the problem. However, I tried as much as possible to avoid or prevent confrontation that would lead to someone being hurt in the first place.

In the eastern part of Nigeria, especially in Igbo society where I was from, education is regarded as the part way or source to many good things in life. The more educated someone is, the higher he or she advances within the society. With better education, one could get higher paid jobs and be able to afford more good things in life. Due to the Nigerian civil war, we lost about four years of schooling. Then after the civil war, which ending in 1970, many people started school all over again where we left off educationally.

My parents gave us the opportunity to learn and be educated, and since they did not have that much education in life, they wanted to give us that opportunity to be educated, and go as far as our brains could take us. To my parents, the sky was the limit as far as education was concerned. To make sure that me and my brothers and sisters get an adequate education, my parents forego many things they wanted in life just to pay our school fees. When they did not have money to pay our school fees, they borrowed money from friends, just to make sure we went to school.

After all the hardships my parents went through just to pay our school fees, I did as much as I could not to disappoint them. I tried as much as possible to make good grades in school with the hope that I would be educated and lived a good life within the society. Most disabled people in Nigeria stayed at home and wallow over their mystery. But my parents did not want me to go through that. They wanted me to be educated and be able to support myself without any body's help. Because of my disability and the weakness of my right leg, I walk with a limp. Without my leg brace, I tend to support that right leg with my hand while walking. Sometimes if my hand got tired and I unconsciously remove it from my leg while walking, I lost my balance and fell.

Different religious organizations have their own schools. Priests manage some religious schools, and in those days, they did not have cohabitation schools. It was either all girls or all boys schools. They did not believe in having cohabitation schools for the fear that the boys might have sex with the girls, and get some of them pregnant. Parents had the options to decide if they wanted to pay just the school fees and have their children go to school from their homes, or they pay for both tuition and boarding fees, and then have their children live in the school dormitories.

My parents chose to send us to catholic boarding schools since we are catholic, and they wanted me to go to the same school with my senior brother, so that he would help me with certain domestic chores. When the Nigerian civil war ended and some students went back to school, many of the schools did not have enough facilities with which to teach the students. Some of the parents sent their children to school with beds, chairs, tables and cooking utensils, and many students cooked their own foods, and then bought some school amenities they used for their studies.

Three years after the civil war ended, the schools received some funds from the state governments and some of the classrooms were furnished with desks and chairs. They also hired some qualified teachers to teach the students. The students that lived in the dormitories did not cook their own foods anymore, because all those amenities were already included when they paid their tuition fees, but they brought their own beds.

One year after the civil war ended, I was admitted in the same school with my senior brother. We lived in the same dormitory with about eighty students. The school had eleven dormitories with about ninety students each. Sometimes at night, when it rained and the whole students went to the classrooms to study, I stayed back and study in the dormitory. The electricity was not reliable, so the students went to the classrooms with lightens to study at night, because they never knew when the light would go off, and would not come back on again for hours or days. Running water was limited and never reliable. It would run for some hours and then shot down for hours or days, so the students had to fetch water from the nearby streams.

My parents lived in a city about one hundred and twenty miles away from the school we attended. My senior brother always looked forward to the school breaks and holidays, because he usually makes some money when he charted some buses to come into the school compound and transported some of the students that lived in the dormitories to different cities where they lived. He arranged to charter some buses about one week before the school ended. Therefore, he knew in advance how many students would be traveling and the number of buses to charter. The profits he made helped us buy some school supplies in the following school year. I stayed with my brother until he graduated and left the school.

When he left the school, I had about two more years to graduate. So in my junior year at the school, I was made a Prefect of one of the freshman classrooms. As a Prefect, I was in charge of the classroom assigned to me. I made sure that the students behave properly or were disciplined, and that they came to the classrooms after dinner to study and do their home works, and then go to bed at 10pm in their individual dormitories.

They were some privileges associated for being a Prefect. As a Prefect I had some of the freshmen students help me with different chores. Some students fetched some water for me when the tap water did not run. They helped me get my food from the cafeteria when I could not go there to eat because of rain. They also helped me with many errands that I could not do because of my disability. With the help of the students, I really enjoyed my senior years at the school.

During my stay at the school, I studied the history of some countries around the world, and the one that picked most of my interest was the United States of America. One of the reasons was that I had seen the movie Roots, which was about the slave trades in America. It was the history of how some people of West Africa, including Nigerians were sold into the slave trades. I learnt that the United State of America was highly developed, and they took care of their disabled peoples. I also learnt that some of their musicians like Steven Wonder, Clearance Carter and Ray Charles were all blind, and were successful musicians. So I said to myself, that if I was able to get to the United States of America, that I stood a chance of living a better normal life with my disability. If you are a disabled person in Nigeria, God help you.

I took my education very seriously and at the end of my senior year, I graduated from high school despite all the physical, social, and psychological difficulties I encountered. However, the thought of coming to the United States of America to study was always in my mind, and how to fulfill that dream at that time was a mystery to me. With my High School Diploma at hand, I took some entrance examinations into different colleges and universities. I tried to gain admission into one of the higher institutions or Universities in Nigeria that were closer to my home, but did not succeed. I took and passed an entrance examination to study Mechanical engineering in one of the Universities in another state. However, I decided not to go to that institution, because of my disability, and the physical hardship I would have encountered.

The reason was that they did not have the infrastructures that were accessible to disabled people. Some of the buildings did not have elevators, and those once that had elevators, brook down so often because of power failure. Nigeria as a country has not taken care of its able bodied people, not to talk about taking care of the disabled people. If you are a disabled person and have a wheelchair, you cannot use them on some of the roads, because the roads are not even good to travel by cars, not to talk about using a wheelchair on them.

While I tried to gain admission into some higher institutions, I applied for a job at the Post Office, and was hired as a Telex Operator. My job at that time was to send telegrams for customers to different parts of the world, who wanted to send instant messages to their friends or families. Those telegrams or instant messages that we transmitted in 1970's had been replaced by emails, which many people have today.

When I worked as a Telex operator, I was able to pay for the leg brace that I wore to work, because it prevented me from falling down frequently. However, the leg brace was made with some inferior materials, that sometimes the weight I put on it, brook the little part of the brace attached into my shoe. It could break any time I walk on it, and sometimes it would break on the street. Once that happened, I had to take the brace off my leg wherever it happened, because that was my only option. It was humiliating, but that was all I could do.

The leg brace had broken too many times that I no longer care about the humiliations it caused me in taken it off wherever it broke. I recalled one incident when I got off work, and walked through the subway tunnel to the other side of the city where I could catch a taxi home. As I walked into the busy tunnel, I noticed that my leg brace was not responding to my walk, so when I took another step, I almost fell, but controlled my balance with the help of a nearby object which I held to support myself. When I looked down at my shoe, I noticed that the portion of my leg brace that attached to the shoe had broken.

Whenever my leg brace brook while I am wearing it, the only option I had to walk again, was to remove the leg brace, and then use my hand to support my right leg while walking. Imagine how embarrassing it was to sit down on the floor of the subway tunnel, and removed my leg brace with all the people walking by and looking at me, and wondering what was wrong with me. Since I knew that was the only option left for me, I did not mind the embarrassment. I just sat down and took the leg brace off. As I was removing the leg brace from my leg, some strangers came by and assisted me. They helped me carry the leg brace to the area where I took a taxi home.

The following day I did not go to work until I fixed my leg brace. When I was in Nigeria, my leg brace brook too many times, but since

I came to the United States of America and made a brand new leg brace, it had never broken with all the fluctuated weights I added to it, and I am very pleased walking with it in confidence.

My senior brother worked at the Post Office too, but in a different department. A few months after he started working at the Post Office, he was transferred to another city. After he transferred to that city, he started planning to come to the United States of America to study. In my mind, I knew that if he succeed in doing so, that I would be the next person to follow his footstep and travel to the United States of America to study. Some of his friends that worked with him at the Post Office had left and were studying in the United States of America. So with the help of some of his friends, he was admitted into some of the colleges in Seattle.

During that period in 1970's, Nigerian currency, the Naira had more value than the United States of America dollar, because the currency was in pounds just like the British Government currency which are in pounds. In those days, the requirement for some of the schools in United State of America was that a student would pay for one year tuition and boarding fees in advance if offered admission.

The student must also take the TOEFL (Test of English as a foreign language) and have a minimum score of 500 before that student could get admission and a visa. With the money my brother saved, he was able to pay one year tuition and boarding fees, and with the TOEL score of 550, he went to the United States of America Embassy and got his visa. He remitted the money to the school and then traveled to the United States of America to study. When he arrived at the school, the school authority took the tuition fees and gave him the rest of the money, which he used to rent an apartment and for foods.

I was very happy the day my senior brother traveled to the United States of America, because I knew that I would follow his footsteps and travel to the United States of America to study. I knew that if I came to the United States of America, that my life would never be the same, because I would be able to have a leg brace that would be strong enough not to break on me while walking. I would be able to drive automatic transmission car with one leg, and do many other things that are accessible to disabled people.

In order to fulfill my educational dreams, I decided that I would come to the United States of America to further my education if given the opportunity. Two years after my senior brother left to study in the United States of America, I started planning seriously to travel to the United States of America to study. First, I took the TOEFL (Test of English as a foreign Language) examination and passed it. Most colleges in the United States of America required the minimum TOEFL score of 500 before getting admission, but my score was 530. Through the help of my brother who was now in the United States of America, I applied for admission to different community colleges in Seattle.

When I applied for admission to some of the Colleges in United State of America, we did not have a telephone at our home in Enugu, but we have telephone at work. Sometimes during my break time or lunch periods, I called my brother and asked him if he heard any information from the school authorities regarding my admission, or if there were any more documents the schools needed from me regarding my admission? One day I called my brother and he told me that one of the colleges, Seattle Central Community College had admitted me, and that he had sent out the admission forms called form I-20 to me.

The day I received my admission documents from Seattle Central Community College, I was not able to sleep, because I was so elated and full of happiness. All I said to myself was that my days living in Nigeria were numbered, once I received a visa to travel to the United States of America. My parents supported my going to the United States of America to further my studies, because they knew that the United States of America would offer me more amenities to support myself as a disabled person.

In those days, getting a United State of America visa was not as difficult as it was today. If you could prove that you have the money and resources to come and study in the United States of America, and with some luck on your side, the United States of America embassy would give you a visa. The reason I said with some luck on your side, was that I had seen some people who had the money and the admission to study in some of the Universities in United States of America, and were not given a visa.

The day I went to get my visa, I took the last airplane that departed from Enugu where we lived to Lagos, which was about forty five minute flight. When the plane took off from the airport and we were on the air, I was so fascinated by the science that was involved in making the plane. How such massive amount of weight could hang in the air and glide to its destination and land. That was mind boggling to me, because that was my first airplane flight experience. When we arrived in Lagos, I stayed at the airport in one of the benches and hoped to catch the early morning taxi to the United States of America embassy. I was only able to catch a few minutes of sleep at a time, because I was conscious of my passport and did not want it to be stolen. I did not eat breakfast before I went to the United States of America embassy that morning.

When I arrived in the United State of America embassy at 5am in the morning, I was the sixth person in line. We waited for three hours before the embassy opened for business at 8am. When it was my turn to receive services, I went to one of the counters and saw one of the embassy staffs. He asked me some questions, which I answered, and then he told me to wait while he left the counter with my passport and the other documents I handed to him.

The period that I waited for him to come back with my passport, was one of the longest anxious times of my life, because I did not know why he left the counter. A few minutes later, he came back, and then handed me my passport and said, congratulations and safe journey to the United States of America. I thanked him, and then left the embassy and headed straight to the airport to see if I could catch any of the flights back home to Enugu. After I was given my visa, I was so happy that I forgot to eat lunch. All I wanted to do was to go home and share the joy and happiness with my family, that I was given a visa to travel to the United States of America and study.

I took the next flight to the city where we lived, and within forty five minutes, I was at the Enugu airport. I had only my carry on luggage, so my check out was easy. I took the taxi, and within ten minutes, I was safely at home. All my family members were so happy for me that I was leaving to go to the United States of America for my studies. The academic year for the school started in September of 1980, but I decided to travel in June, so that I would spend some time with my brother and his family before the fall quarter started.

When I went to the travel agency to book for my flight to United States of America, I told them to find me the cheapest airline to travel to Seattle in the United States of America. The cheapest airline they offered me was Aeroflot airline. They told me that I would stop over in some countries, before going to the United States of America. I said fine, as long as I arrived at my destination, which was the city of Seattle in United States of America.

I later found out that Aeroflot airline was the USSR (Union of Soviet Socialist Republics) airline, and USSR is now Russia, which in those days was a communist country airline. The airline only flies to communist countries and to some other countries, which were nonaligned nations. They fly to communist countries, which have an affiliation with USSR, and to countries, which did not have an allegiance to either United States of America or USSR.

After I booked my flight to travel to the United States of America, I started counting down the number of days I had left to stay in Nigeria, and I was sleeping very well at night. I only told some of my closest friends that I was about to travel to the United States of America to further my education. On the day of my travel, some of my friends and family members came to the airport and wished me a safe journey. I took a flight from Enugu to Lagos, and since my flight to the United States of America was to leave at 11pm that night, I decided to stay at the airport until the departure of my flight.

When we started boarding the airplane, we all stood in line as the flight attendants checked our boarding passes. When it was my turn to board the plane, I handed them my boarding pass and they pointed me to the row where my seat was. I went and sat there. A few minutes after we took off, dinner was served, and I really enjoyed the food I was given. A few hours after we left Lagos, we arrived at Libya airport. Some passenger got off the airplane while some boarded the plane. The airplane took off, and our next destination in my flight itinerary was Amsterdam. In Amsterdam, we changed flights and then I boarded Delta airline to the United States of America.

I really enjoyed my flight from Amsterdam to New York, where I boarded another plane to Seattle. On the airplane from Amsterdam to New York, I watched some movies, and might have dozed off some couple of times while watching those movies. There was a time one beautiful flight attendant tapped me on my shoulder and I woke up, and noticed that we were been served different kinds of foods and drinks. She showed me two kinds of sandwiches and told me to take one. She said that they had hamburgers with fries and the other one was hot dogs with fries.

I told her that I did not want a hot dog, so I took the hamburger instead. The sentiment that ran through my head when she said hot dog was so weird. I said to myself, so I was I going to a country where they eat dog meats. I did not ask the flight attendant what she meant by hot dog, since she gave me the option to choose from two kinds of foods.

When I we arrived at New York airport, we were checked in by the customs agency for the validation of our passports and visas. Then I took the airport Train to the terminal where I boarded the flight to Seattle airport. Our plane arrived at Seattle airport safely and I checked out my luggage. A few minutes later, I saw my brother and his wife waiting for me. We hugged and exchanged some greetings. My brother loaded my luggage in the truck of the car and we all got into the car and drove off.

During our journey to my brother's house, I asked him if he ate hot dogs. He told me yes, I told him that we never ate dog meat in Nigeria, why did he came over here and started eating dog meat? I told him the experience I had with the flight attendant about hot dog on the airplane. They busted out laughing, and they told me that the hot dog sandwich did not mean that it was cooked with dog meat. They said that it was only a name given to that kind of sandwich, and that the meat was cooked with beef meat and some with pork meat. Anyway, that was my awkward welcome experience in the United States of America, and that was not the last.

One other embarrassing incident happened to me in school after I finished taking one of my classes with one of my American female friends. She was waving goodbye to me as she walked away. However, how she was gesturing her hand, looked as if she was inviting me to come towards her. As I approached her, she asked me if I forgot something, I told her that I thought that she was inviting me to come towards her. She laughed and said no. She said that all she was doing was waving goodbye to me. Since then, I had learned many America ways of life and cultures.

Before I came to the United States of America, I had in mind to study Computer Science, Accountancy or Mathematics. I also wanted to earn the highest degree education could offer, which was a doctorate degree. But at the end, my ambition did not materialize the way I envisioned it, because of some of the misfortunes I encountered in my life.

When I first came to the United states of America, my parents sent some school fees to me, but when I became a permanent resident of the United States of America and was working, I told them to stop sending school fees to me because I could support myself. I found out that the school fees were cheaper at community colleges than at a four year college or the University. Since I was already a student at Seattle Central Community College, I decided to take most of my courses there before I transferred to a four year college or university.

I took most of my courses in the main building of Seattle Central Community College. The buildings were constructed in a way that when it rained or snowed and I was inside the building, I would complete all my school activities and would not feel those weather conditions, because the general areas of the buildings were covered with some sunshine rooftops that allowed the sun rays into the buildings.

The students were friendly, but some of the teachers were not, because some of them were not used to the European kind of English that I spook. It took a while before some of the teachers gave me a nice grade in some of those courses that required writing an essay. I scored some of my lowest grades in those essay courses, but I tried to make up my lower Grade Point Average score with those courses that I knew very well.

I love mathematics and I tried to do my best in those mathematics courses that I registered for each quarter. Some of my professors sometimes wondered how a disabled black person like me had the mind to think logically just as I did in their classes. Some of them found one fault or another just to give me a low grade. After studying for about two years at Seattle Central Community College, I transferred my grades and credit scores to the University of Washington in 1983. Since I did not have enough money to pay for my school fees, I applied for some financial aid programs. I was given some financial aid, including work study programs and some student loans. All those financial aids were given to me on the condition that I had to maintain a two point minimum Grade point average (GPA).

University of Washington is a big school with over thirty eight thousand students. The university campus is like a small city of its own inside the city of Seattle. What I disliked the most about the university was the distance between the buildings where I took my classes. Going from one class to another within the fifteen minute break allowed to change classes were a big hassle to me, because of my disability. Sometimes before I could walk to my next class, the professor had already started lecturing.

One day I came in late for a class, and one of the students I was chatting with told me about the disabled shuttle program at the university. She told me that the university had Vans that took disabled students to and from different classes within the fifteen minutes time interval allowed for them to make it to their classes on time. So I enrolled in the shuttle program, and that minimized the hardship I had in walking those distances for class change, and I was on time for my classes.

I thought that attending the University of Washington would bring me closer to my dreams, but boy was I wrong. I never envisaged the kind of obstacle and racism that I encountered when I declared that mathematics was my major. Some of the professors gave me low grades in mathematics, as if to say, that the courses that I was taken was meant only for some brains, and that I was in the wrong class or rather pursuing the wrong profession.

In fact, what we had at the University of Washington and in Seattle in general was what I called silent discrimination. In short, I call it, killing me softly kind of discrimination. It was the kinds of discriminations, in which some people would chat and laugh with you, as you became acquaintances, friends, coworkers, and your employers etc. However, deep inside their minds and behind your back, they are talking stupid things about you, degrading you and figuratively killing you softly, by preventing you in progressing in whatever endeavors you are pursuing in life.

Take for example, the quarter that I registered and took mathematics124 calculus. Half way into the quarter, the Professor fell sick and did not complete teaching the course for that quarter. A teacher's assistant called TA, took over the teaching of the course and stated that he would give us twenty homework assignments, which would count as one third of the final grades at the end of the quarter.

At the end of that quarter, the teacher's assistant gave us two options where to pick up our examination papers. He said that we could pick up our papers in his office, or he would leave them outside his office door. He gave us a document, which we signed and indicated which options we preferred. He told us that the examination papers he kept in his office would not be available for pick up until the start of the following quarter, since he would not be in his office. I signed that I wanted my papers kept in his office, so that if there were any questions for me to ask him, I would do that when I came to pick up my papers.

Remember the TA said that homework assignments would count as one third of the final grades of the course. I did all my homework assignments and took the final examination. However, would you believe that this TA gave me a zero grade at the end of that quarter, despite the fact that I did all my homework assignments, which the TA said, would count as one third of the final grades of the course. Just by doing the homework assignments, would have earned me some kind of a passing grade. However, the zero grade he gave me indicated that I failed the course, and that lowered my Grade Point Average score drastically.

When the next quarter began, I went to the TA's office to pick up my examination papers, and he told me that he did not find my papers. I asked him for my last homework assignment papers, he told me that did not find those copies either. I asked him if he could grade me on the nineteen homework assignments that he had already corrected and gave back to me. He said no, that since he did not see and corrected my twentieth homework assignment copies, that he would not give me a final grade for my homework assignments.

I complained to the school authority that the TA (Teacher Assistant) gave me a zero grade, because he lost my examination papers. They told me that they would not investigate it, because the last decision for the grades in the courses depended on the teachers. I went back and talked to the teacher again, and asked him what he wanted me to do, so that I could get a decent grade for the hard work I put into that class. He told me that he would give me another test, and that if I scored 60%, that he would give me a passing grade. That incident had already dragged on into my second year at the University. When I finally took the test, the TA gave me 56%, and since I was 4% less than the 60% he wanted me to score, he did not change the zero grade he gave me for the course.

I needed that mathematics 124 calculus to graduate, and if I retook the course at the University of Washington, I had to pay higher school fees for that same course. Since school fees were cheaper at North Seattle Community College, I went there and enrolled in summer school the following year, and then retook the same mathematics 124 calculus again. At the end of the quarter, I received a C grade for the same course, which the TA at the University of Washington gave me a zero grade.

The C grade I received for that same course indicated that the TA at the University of Washington would have given me at least a passing grade or better in that course. Anyway, the zero grade given to me by that TA, lowered my GPA scores (grade point average) all through my student years at the University.

Another incident happened to me when I took mathematics 205 and

302 algebra. The Professor that taught those courses always gave me lower grades, no matter how good I did in the courses. The reason was that he wanted me to use the long method, which he taught us in class to solve the mathematics problems. He also taught us the short and logical method we could use to solve the same problem, and get the same answer, and it was not time consuming.

With the limited time given during test periods to complete the mathematics problems, using the short method to solve the problems were better and faster. When he gave us those tests, he did not state which method to use, so I used the short method approach to solve the problems, because it was faster and saved some time during the examinations. If he had stated that we should use the long method, which he taught us, obviously I would have used it, to avoid getting a failed grade. Technically, those two methods achieved the same goal, which was to get the right answers to the same mathematics problems.

When I met the Professor and asked him why he gave me lower grades for those courses? He told me that he wanted me to use the very long method that he taught us to solve those mathematics problems. I explained to him why I used the short method to solve the problems, and that the logic in using the short or the long methods were the same. I told him that he did not stipulate on the test that he wanted us to use only the long method approach to solve the mathematics problems, so we were free to use whatever methods we desired to solve the mathematics problems. But if he had stated that he wanted us to use the long method, that I would have used it. He told me that he understood the logic behind the method that I used, because it was faster and to the point. However, he insisted that he wanted me to use the long method approach, and that he was sorry that it was not stated on the tests.

In mathematics, you could use whatever method you knew that could best solve the problems as long as there were logical, and you get the correct answer to the problems. Anyway, I ended up with C grades in those courses. I went through a period of hardship when I was a student at the University of Washington before I graduated. Throughout my student years at the University of Washington, my Grade point average scores (GPA) never improved after I received that zero grade in Mathematics 124 calculus, and the lower grades in Mathematics 205 and 302 algebra courses. In fact, I received two probation notices in autumn quarter of 1984 and autumn quarter of 1985, when my GPA scores were below 2.0 points.

Whenever a student was on probation, that student had to improve their Grade Point Average scores to 2.0 points or higher, or risk being dropped from the university program. Therefore, when I did not maintain 2.0 GPA score in subsequent academic years, I received a dropped notice in winter of 1986, and was no longer a student at the University of Washington. I was not allowed to register for any class at the university. For me to be reinstated into the university, I had to register at another school, have a better Grade Point Average score, and then reapply to be reinstated into the University and in Mathematics department.

My Social Welfare life

Now let us step back and try to figure out, if there were some factors that might have contributed to my emotional distress, and lack of concentration on my school activities. In August 1983 when I was injured at my job at Industrial Laundry Company, I went through some emotional and stressful period of my life, because I also sued the company for discrimination. I received workers compensation benefits every month from August 1983 to February 1985 after my injury. Sometimes my benefits stopped abruptly without adequate reasons. It was very stressful to live without any money, and very difficult to plan ahead on what to do with my life, when I did not have any money to pay my bills.

By November 1985, I had already exhausted my workers compensation benefits, and was no longer receiving any money from the state Industrial insurance. I would have been homeless, but fortunately, before I exhausted my workers compensation benefits, I applied for an apartment at the disabled housing complexes, through the Seattle Housing Authority in 1983.

In the early part of 1984, I was given a one bedroom unit at one of the disabled housing complexes in South Seattle. It was an eight story building with elevators, and I lived in the third floor of the building. Only disabled peoples occupied these units, and we paid the rents based on how much we earned as incomes. This implied that, if I did not earn any income, then I did not pay any rent. However, if I had any income, then I paid the rent based on my income.

During those periods that I received workers compensation benefits, I went to school and paid my school fees with the assistance I received from the financial aid programs of the University of Washington. But when I did not maintain 2.0 Grade Point Average score, my financial aid was stopped.

With many obstacles in my life, sometimes I tried to quit struggling to better my life. However, who would take care of me if I did not take care of myself. By December 1986 and beginning of fall quarter of 1987, I was so broke financially that I did not have any money to feed myself. Therefore, I went to the Department of Social and Health Services and applied for assistance. My application was approved, and I was given eighty seven ($87.00) dollars of food stamps every month for the next eight months. Before the end of the eight months, I went to the department again for an evaluation and for more assistance. Those food stamps given to me were used exclusively to buy foods, and no money was given to me.

My food stamp identification number and other documents given to me for food stamp eligibility

I changed my name from Chukwubike Nworjih to Chibike Nwabude, and I explained the reason for the change in the chapters where I discussed about my father.

You will need to have the attached IDENTIFICATION CARD with you whenever you obtain food coupons or do your food shopping. Please sign the Identification Card and keep it in a safe place so that it will be available each time you go to get your coupons or buy food. If your spouse, a responsible member of your household or an authorized representative designated by you will be picking up your coupons or buying your groceries, PRINT his/her name on the reverse of this card in the space provided. BOTH OF YOU MUST THEN SIGN THE CARD.

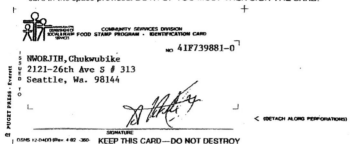

COMMUNITY SERVICES DIVISION
FOOD STAMP PROGRAM · IDENTIFICATION CARD

NO 41F739881-0

NWORJIH, Chukwubike
2121-26th Ave S # 313
Seattle, Wa. 98144

< (DETACH ALONG PERFORATIONS)

SIGNATURE

DSHS 12-0400 (Rev. 4-82 -360-   KEEP THIS CARD—DO NOT DESTROY

NOTICE OF PLANNED ACTION (INCAPACITY)

LOCAL OFFICE	TELEPHONE
Rainier	721-4788
CASE NUMBER 41-U-739881-0	DATE 9/17/87

PLEASE SEE THE SECTION(S) CHECKED BELOW FOR IMPORTANT INFORMATION REGARDING YOUR ASSISTANCE. ALSO SEE IMPORTANT INFORMATION ON THE REVERSE SIDE OF THIS FORM.

Chukwubike Nwobyih
2121 - 26th Ave. So. #313
Seattle, WA 98144

IF YOU HAVE QUESTIONS ABOUT THIS ACTION, TELEPHONE ME AT THE NUMBER SHOWN AT THE TOP RIGHT.

YOU HAVE BEEN RECEIVING ASSISTANCE BECAUSE YOU WERE FOUND TO BE INCAPACITATED FROM GAINFUL EMPLOYMENT. THE PURPOSE OF THIS NOTICE IS TO INFORM YOU THAT YOUR FINANCIAL AND MEDICAL ASSISTANCE WILL BE TERMINATED EFFECTIVE _9-30-87_

THE REASON FOR THIS ACTION IS:

☒ We have not received a response to our request for current medical information. Because any further award of assistance must be based in part on current medical evidence, we cannot establish that your incapacity continues to exist. (WAC 388-37-032(4), 388-24-065)

☐ The medical evidence we have received so far is inconclusive. It does not adequately inform us whether or not you are still incapacited. Therefore, as of this date, we cannot establish that your incapacity continues to exist. (WAC 388-37-032(4), 388-24-065)

☐ Based on our consideration of current medical evidence along with previously submitted medical information, we conclude that you are no longer incapacitated. (WAC 388-37-035, 388-24-065) The specific reason for this conclusion is as follows:

_____

In addition, one of the findings checked below was made in your case:

☐ The medical information establishes that there has been clear improvement in your case since the determination of incapacity.

☐ The medical information establishes that there was an error in the prior determination of incapacity.

ADDITIONAL INFORMATION ABOUT YOUR CASE:

_____
_____
_____

YOUR FOOD STAMPS WILL BE:

☐ CONTINUED WITH NO CHANGES.

☐ TERMINATED, EFFECTIVE _____

☒ CHANGED, EFFECTIVE _10-1_ PRESENT ALLOTMENT $ _37.00_ PROPOSED ALLOTMENT $ _87.00_
These will terminate on 11-30, 87

▮▮▮▮▮▮▮▮▮▮
FST

DSHS 14-39A(X) (6-85) OX A-212

SEE IMPORTANT INFORMATION ON REVERSE SIDE REGARDING YOUR FAIR HEARING RIGHTS

NOTICE OF ACTION

LOCAL OFFICE	TELEPHONE
Rainier	721-4775
CASE NUMBER	**DATE**
41-F-239881-0	11/25/80

FST ▓▓▓▓▓▓

Chukwubike Nworji
2121-26th Ave S. #3B
Seattle, Wa 98144

Please refer to the blocks checked below for actions taken or information required on your food stamp case.

1. ☒ You are certified eligible for the Food Stamp Program from _12/01/80_ to _01/31/88_
   Your food stamp benefits will be:
   a) _87.00_ for _12/80_   c) _____ for _____
   b) _____ for _____   d) _____ for _____

   ☒ **NOTICE OF EXPIRATION:**
   Your food stamp certification period expires on _01/31/88_ . In order to continue to be eligible for and receive food stamps, you must complete and submit a new application. Part 1 of your application must be received in our office by _____

2. ☐ Your application for food stamps received on _____ has been
   ☐ Denied   ☐ Withdrawn   ☐ Pended
   If your case was Pended, see block 7 below for what information you need to provide:
   If you submit the information by _____ you will not have to reapply.

3. ☐ You sent in a change of circumstances. See block 7 below for the required information and/or verification: We need this information by _____

4. ☒ Because you needed food stamp benefits right away, we postponed asking you to give us certain information. We now need you to bring or mail in the following information no later than _12-10-80_ . See block 7 below for explanation.

5. ☐ You'll receive an increase/decrease in monthly food stamp benefits from $_____ to $_____
   beginning in the month of _____ because (see block 7 below):

6. ☐ Your case will be closed effective _____ . You are no longer eligible for food stamps because (see block 7 below):

7. ☒ See BLOCK _4_ above: _provide current bank statement._

Please read the back of this form as it informs you of your rights.

DSHS 12-90 (X) (Rev 9-85) OX A-204

NOTICE OF ACTION

LOCAL OFFICE	TELEPHONE
Rainier	*721-4782*
CASE NUMBER	DATE
41F-739881-0	*01/22/88*

F.ST.

WASHINGTON STATE
DEPARTMENT OF
SOCIAL & HEALTH
SERVICES

Chibike Nwalude
2121 26th Ave S. #313
Seattle, Wa. 98144

Please refer to the blocks checked below for actions taken or information required on your food stamp case.

1. ☒ You are certified eligible for the Food Stamp Program from *02/01/88* to *04/30/88*
   Your food stamp benefits will be:
   a) *87.00* for *Monthly Benefits unless Circumstances*
   Change for _____ d) _____ for _____

   NOTICE OF EXPIRATION:
   ☐ Your food stamp certification period expires on _____. In order to continue to be eligible for and receive food stamps, you must complete and submit a new application. Part 1 of your application must be received in our office by _____

2. ☐ Your application for food stamps received on _____ has been
   ☐ Denied   ☐ Withdrawn   ☐ Pended
   If your case was Pended, see block 7 below for what information you need to provide:
   If you submit the information by _____ you will not have to reapply.

3. ☐ You sent in a change of circumstances. See block 7 below for the required information and/or verification: We need this information by _____

4. ☐ Because you needed food stamp benefits right away, we postponed asking you to give us certain information. We now need you to bring or mail in the following information no later than _____ See block 7 below for explanation.

5. ☐ You'll receive an increase/decrease in monthly food stamp benefits from $_____ to $_____ beginning in the month of _____ because (see block 7 below):

6. ☐ Your case will be closed effective _____. You are no longer eligible for food stamps because (see block 7 below):

7. ☐ See BLOCK _____ above: _____

Please read the back of this form as it informs you of your rights.

DSHS 12-90 (X) (Rev 9/86) QX A-204

When I received those food stamps, I was so ashamed to use them to buy groceries. I lived in the south of Seattle, so what I did was that any time I wanted to buy some groceries, I traveled some few miles away from my neighborhood to the grocery stores in the west, east or north of Seattle. Because I was afraid, that some people or some friends that I knew might recognize me using food stamps to buy some foods.

When I was in the grocery stores, I went to different aisles and took the food items and goods that I wanted to buy. Then I went to one corner of the store or in one of the aisles, and calculated approximately how much the food items would cost. I tore out that amount of food stamp coupons from the booklet, and have them ready in my pocket. The next thing that I did, was to make sure that the counter where I went to pay for those items have fewer people on the line or there was nobody on the line. Also, I made sure that the line did not have any body that I knew, and that I did not know the Cashier. Once the cashier finished scanning those items for payments, I pulled that amount of food stamp coupons, out from my pocket and gave them to the cashier without attracting too much attention to myself.

The government might have been aware that using food stamp coupons to buy foods might have caused some embarrassment to some people, and to save some operating cost, they decided to stop using food stamp coupons. Today the amount of food stamps vouchers given to someone are credited in a card that looks like a credit card, and it requires a pin number or an identification number to assess the amounts on the card. Therefore, when someone with a food stamp card is at the counter to pay for food items, he or she might be using food stamp credit cards, and the person behind him or her would not know that they are using food stamps.

The eighty seven ($87.00) dollars of food stamps per month given to me was not enough. To receive more assistance, I sometimes went to some food banks, and received some donated foods. Just as I was ashamed in using food stamp coupons to buy foods, I did not want anyone that I knew to see me going to food banks to get some foods.

Therefore, what I did was that, since I lived in the south of Seattle, I went to some of the food banks in the north, east or west of Seattle, just to avoid the recognition by someone I knew. That was more than twenty seven years ago.

Guess what, one day I went to the food bank in north Seattle to get some foods. Just as I pulled my car to park in one of the meters about one block away from the front of the food bank building, I saw a car that looked like that of my friend, turned into the parking lot of the food bank building. That friend of mine also lived about twenty blocks from where I lived in south Seattle. He did not see me when I parked my car. Therefore, I sat in my car and waited, just to make sure if that was really my friend that I saw. Sure enough, it was him.

After about sixteen minutes, I got out of my car and went into the food bank building. I pretended as if I was looking for someone, because there was another office there. Just as I approached the receptionist, I saw my friend with two bags of foods in his hands. I said hello to him, and he asked me what I was doing there? I told him that I was looking for a friend, but that I did not know if she worked in that building or the next building.

Since my friend had some bags of foods in his hands, there was no way he would deny that he was there to get some foods. He told me that he never expected to see someone that he knew there, and that was the reason he drove all the way from south Seattle to north Seattle, just to avoid the recognition by someone he knew. He told me that he had some financial problems, and that was the reason he came there and received some donated foods.

Anyway, since I did not want him to know that I was there to take some donated foods, I chatted with him as we walked to where he parked his car. He opened the truck of his car, put the bags of foods in the truck, and then walked towards the driver's side of his car. Once he got into his car, I said goodbye to him, and then walked to where I parked my car.

As he drove off, I also drove off, because I knew he might be watching me through his rear view mirror. As he drove through the traffic light, I drove to the next block and then turned into the next street closer to the food bank building. Once I was sure that I had lost sight of my friend's car, I drove back to the food bank building, parked my car, and then walked into the building. I picked up two bags of donated foods and then left.

Do not get me wrong, there was nothing wrong for someone who needed some assistance to use food stamp coupons to buy some foods or to go to food banks to get some foods. I was used to working and paying for my foods with my money, but some circumstances brought me to those predicaments that I had to depend on government handouts. I did not want to depend on handouts to support myself. I wanted to work to support myself.

However, the government instituted those programs to help individuals who are in need of assistance, to be able to use the food stamp coupons to buy some food items, or go to the food banks and get some donated foods. It is a temporary assistance, until that individual is able to support him or herself again. In my case, I went there as a last resort just because I was in a desperate need of some help. I knew that was not how I wanted to support myself.

The years 1986 and 1987 would go down as one of the worst years of my life, because the University of Washington dropped me from their program, I lost my student financial aid assistance, I supported myself with food stamps, and I vigorously looked for a job, but could not get any job.

The first discriminations experience I had at my former job was so dramatic and demoralizing, that it took me a while to regain some confidence in my own abilities, and rebuilt my life again. However, the effect of discrimination and its stress, was reflected in the grades I received at school, because my GPA scores (grade point average) was always lower than that of an average student. With many obstacles in my life, sometimes it was very difficult to deal with, and sometimes I tried to quit struggling while trying to better my life. Again, who would take care of me if I did not take care of myself?

During those periods, the discrimination lawsuit I filed against my former company, Industrial Laundry Company, was settled in July 1986, and I used the money I received to pay down some of my debts. I wanted to use the remaining amount to pay for my school fees for the 1987 academic year. However, how could I with good conscience live with myself, without helping my mother who was terribly sick? Therefore, I used part of the money, bought a flight ticket to Nigeria, and visited my mother who was very sick at that time.

The day I went back home to Nigeria and saw how sick, my mother was, I used part of that money to pay her flight ticket to visit the United States of America for some medical treatments. I also remodeled some parts of the house where they lived in Nigeria. I stayed for about three weeks in Nigeria, and by the time I came back to the United States of America, the money was all gone. Then sometime in 1987, my sick mother visited the United States of America, and stayed with my senior brother in Seattle.

When my mother had her knee surgery to replace one of her knee joint, she came and stayed with me, because she could not use a wheelchair to walk around in my brother's house. My building had elevators, because it was built for disabled people. Since I was not working at that time, I used those periods to take care of my sick mother.

I never told my mother that I was not working, and that I was dropped from the University of Washington study programs. I also never told her that I used food stamps to buy some of the foods we ate. The reason was that I did not want her to bother about my welfare. I also told my brothers and sisters not to discuss my situations with our mother.

Though with motherly instinct, she had her suspicion that something must be wrong with me, because she asked me sometimes why I stayed home quite often. I made up some excuses that I took a long vacation or that the doctor gave me some days off. My brothers and sisters were very supportive, because they knew that I was not working, but they did not know that I was dropped from the University of Washington study programs, because of low grade point average scores. They sent some money to me every month to use in feeding and taking care of our mother, and that was how I was able to get some gas money for my car.

The second stage of my education experience

I had only twenty two course credits to graduate from the University of Washington, and I had no money to pay for my school fees. However, I knew that the only way for me to better my life and get out of that welfare predicament, was to finish my education, get a job and then support myself.

Since the University of Washington had already dropped me from their programs, and I could not register for any course, I talked to some of the university counselors about my situations, and some of them advised me to take some time off from the school, because I was stressed out. They told me that if I happened to come back to school again, that I would be refreshed and ready for the challenges ahead.

One of the counselors advised me to change my major from mathematics to economics, or to some other courses. She told me quote "there was no way you would ever graduate with a mathematics degree". I told her that I love mathematics, because I could understand it easily and logically. I also told her that since I was already admitted in mathematics department, that I would not like to change my major.

After that discussion I had with that counselor, I was more determined than ever to graduate with a degree in mathematics, just to prove to her and everyone else that what they told me that quote "there was no way you would ever graduate with a mathematics degree" was wrong. Therefore, what I did was that I sold some of the valuable things I had, like one of my watches and necklaces, just to raise enough money to register for one course of four credit loads.

In spring quarter of 1986, I registered for Introduction to FORTRAN programming course (Engineering 141) for four credits, at the University of Washington Extension College. It was a branch of the University of Washington, where students took correspondence courses, and study at their own pace. The students at the college used the university library, and the teacher's assistants were there to help the students with any questions they have. At the end of the quarter, I received a 3.1 Grade Point Average score, for the course.

When I contacted the University of Washington registration office, and showed them the grade I had in Engineering 141 course, I was told to apply for reinstatement into the University of Washing study programs. My application was approved, and I was reinstated back into the Mathematics department of the University of Washington.

THE LETTER THAT I ATTACHED TO THE "PETITION FOR REINSTATEMENT" FORM DATED 7/26/86

> I wish to apply for reinstatement for fall quarter 1986. When I had a low Grade Point Average (GPA) score, and was dropped by the school, I explained the circumstances that lead to the low grade that I got (that was my poor health and lack of concentration), but the committee told me to take some time off my studies.

Had it been that I was given the opportunity to register for spring quarter, I would have improved my GPA, because I knew that I was feeling much better health wise than I was when I had those low grades.

Having been dropped from school, and also prevented from registering for spring quarter, I wanted to convince myself that I should have improved my GPA, had it been I was given the opportunity, so I went and registered for Engineering 141course at the University of Washington Extension for spring quarter 1986. At the end of the quarter, I scored a 3.1 grade point on the course. Though, it was below what I expected, but it proved that I was ready for spring quarter and was not given the opportunity to register.

Please I am begging that I be given the opportunity to register for fall quarter 1986, since the low GPA, I got was due to my poor health. Now that I am feeling much better, I think that if giving the opportunity that I will do better. Thanks

Yours faithfully

Chukwubike Nworjih

PETITION FOR REINSTATEMENT
Please do not write on the reverse side

Approval of this petition does not guarantee registration for any particular quarter. To be eligible to return to the University, the student must complete a former student application in the Registrar's Office by the application closing date and present an approved reinstatement petition. A student who is anticipating reinstatement may file a former student application before his reinstatement is approved.

Date __7/21/86__

Name __Chukwubike   Nworjih__ Telephone ____

Address __2121   26th Ave South #313 seattle 98144__

Last attended University of Washington __Winter__ Quarter 19 __86__ Student Number __XXXX615__

Any college subsequently attended _____ Dates ____

I submit the following information in support of my case for reinstatement commencing _____ Quarter 19 ____

Enclosed or rather attached is my application for reinstatement.

Reinstated by committee

This space is reserved for Dean's action

Reinstatement Granted ☒ Denied ☐ Deferred ☐ Effective __Autumn__ Quarter 19 __86__

In College of __Arts & Sciences__ Major __Mathematics__

Date __7/29/86__

UW 20-514   Signature of Dean

After my reinstatement into the University of Washington study programs, I did not have any money to pay for my school fees, because I was not working, and I did not have any financial aid from the university. At that time, I was more determined to do everything I could do to graduate, because I had only twenty two course credit loads left to graduate with a degree in mathematics.

Therefore, I decided that the best thing for me to do was to go to school anyway. I went to the Administration office of the university, and registered for the courses that I wanted to take for that winter quarter of 1987, without paying for them. I woke up every morning, went to school, took those classes, and then took all the homework assignments and examinations for those courses.

The university had a deadline when every student had to pay for all the classes they registered for the quarters. When that date approached, I did not have any money to pay for my school fees, and my name was dropped from the final class rosters of all those courses that I registered for that quarter. Once a student's name was dropped from the final roster of the courses, the teachers were given the official names of all the students that registered in their classes, and they were not allowed to admit any student whose name was not on the official roster to study in their classes, and take any examinations for those courses.

However, I was so determined to go to school, because that was the only way, I could get myself out of the welfare predicaments. So in the subsequent quarters of winter, summer and autumn of 1987, I registered for some courses, and since I did not have any money to pay for the courses, I was later dropped from the final class rosters.

In the quarters that I registered for some courses, but was dropped from the class rosters, I told the teachers that taught those courses my predicaments. I told them that I had no money to pay for my school fees, and that I was on welfare assistance programs. I also told them that I had been looking for a job, but had not gotten any job.

Now that the professors were aware of my situations, they allowed me to come into their classes, took the homework assignments and the examinations. They told me that at the end of the quarters, that they would withhold my grades in their offices, since I was not officially registered for the courses. If I had paid my school fees, and the courses were officially registered, my grades and credit scores would have been entered into my transcripts, and counted towards my graduation. I took a total of six courses in winter, summer and autumn quarters of 1987, without paying for the school fees. Below is the list of courses I took with the grades I received.

The grades I received for the courses

Courses	Number of credits	Quarter Taken in 1987	Grades
Economic 201	5	Winter	2.3
Mathematics 303	3	Winter	2.7
Mathematics 407	3	Winter	2.7
Mathematics 420	3	Summer	3.0
Oceanography 101	5	Summer	2.0
Mathematics 427	3	Autumn	3.0
Total credits	22		

As the academic year of 1987 was ending, I knew that if I did not pay the school fees for those courses that I took, and have them officially registered and recorded in my transcripts, that I would lose them. Then all the hard works and efforts that I invested in those courses to earn those grades would be wasted. The reason was that, the University of Washington policies, stated that all courses and grades earned in any academic year had to be registered and recorded in that academic year.

Fortunately for me as the 1987 academic year was about to end, I received three thousand nine hundred and eighty six dollars ($3986.00) settlement money from my car insurance company, for the car accident I had in 1986. I wanted to use three thousand dollars (**$3000.00)** of that money to pay for those courses that I took, and have them officially entered in my transcripts. I went to the school authority and told them that I took some classes in summer, autumn and winter quarters of 1987, and that I wanted to pay for the courses, and have the grades recorded in my transcripts. They told me that it was too late to register past quarter grades, especially when my grades were two to three quarters past the current quarter.

The supervisor in the transcript and grade recording office of the university, told me to go and talk to Mr. Frank Byrdwell Jr. who was the Assistant Registrar of the school at that time. They told me that if he allowed me to register for the courses, that they would honor his request.

For me to present my case to Mr. Frank Bydwell Jr, I knew that I needed some convincing evidence about my situation. So I went to the six Professors that gave me the opportunity to take those courses in their classes, and gave them the cards used to add and drop courses, to sign that I took those courses from them. The add and drop course cards are used by students to add the courses they wanted to take for the quarter, or to drop any course they did not want to take.

The professors signed the cards and wrote the quarters that I took the courses in their classes. I wrote a request letter to register those courses, and attached the six signed add course cards from the Professors to it. In the letter, I explained that I was on welfare, and that I did not have any money to pay for my school fees. I also explained that the reason I took the courses was to graduate, and get out of my welfare predicament. Here is what I wrote in the letter.

In summer, autumn and winter quarters of 1987, I did not have any money to pay for my school fees, and I was on welfare assistant (copies of my welfare assistant letters enclosed). I had only twenty two course credits to graduate, so I went to school during the above mentioned quarters, took some courses and received some grades for those courses.

Officially, I did not register for those courses, because I did not have the money to pay for the courses. Please, I knew that what I did (that is, by going to school without officially registering for the courses) was illegal according to the school policies. But I knew that the only way I could help myself and get out from the welfare assistant, and be useful to myself and the society, was to go to school, graduate and then get a job. So that was the reason I took those courses, hoping that I will one day get the money to pay for my school fees, and have the courses entered in my transcripts.

Please I have come up with the money to pay for those courses I took through the help of my friends. I am begging you to please, allow me to pay for those courses, so that my different Professors can send my grades to the grading office and have them recorded in my transcripts.

Enclosed are the add and drop course cards for those courses I took that were signed by my different Professors. I am very sorry for all the inconvenience my action has caused you and all the people concern. Since these are all the courses that I needed to graduate, I am begging you, to please allow me to pay for these courses. Thanks in anticipation.

Yours Sincerely

Chibike Nwabude

The first time I went to Mr. Frank Byrdwell Jr. office, he was not there. The following day, I went to his office and told him my predicaments, and handed him the letter I wrote about registering the courses I took, with the signed add/drop course cards from the Professors. He read the letter, and then sat there for a few minutes without saying a word. Then he stared at me for a few more seconds, and said that he was captivated by my stories. He told me that in the number of years that he had worked in the school, that he had never heard or seen anything like what I did and just told him.

He told me that what the Professors deed was unlawful, and against the school policies, but since they have already allowed me into their classes, took the examinations and received grades for the courses, that he would help me in any way possible to see that those grades were recorded in my transcripts.

He told me that the only way that he would help me, was for me to go and meet all of the six Professors for those courses that I took, and have them give me a signed written letter that stated the courses, and grades they gave me for each of the courses. He also told me that it would be difficult to convince the school authorities to allow me to pay for those courses, since the record entries for those quarters that I took those courses had closed.

It took me a while to track down each of the Professors, because it was almost one year since I took the courses from them. However, once I was in contact with any of the Professors, they were willing to give me a signed written letter to give to the school authority. Here are the copies of the signed letters from the six Professors.

To Registrar   2/29/88

From ████████████████████ Lecturer Mathematics

          ()

Mr Chibike Nwabude Completed My course
in Math 427 Autumn Quarter 1987 .
Obtaining a grade of 3.0 to be awarded to him

          ████████████████████

          746-XXXX

2/29/88

To the Registrar

From

Re   Chukwubike Jworjih
       participation in Ocean 101   Summer Quarter 1987

Mr Nworjih was an attending student in the Ocean 101
class summer quarter 1987. He participated fully in this
course by being in class and doing all assigned work
as well as taking all the exams. His name was not on
my final grade sheet because of financial reasons between
him and the University.
    I am very willing to assign a grade of 2.0 to him
for his efforts if the University can arrange for this
grade to be recorded.

                          Sincerely,

                          Research Assoc. Prof. School of Oceanography
                                Campus   WB-10

phone   543-XXXX

UNIVERSITY OF WASHINGTON
SEATTLE, WASHINGTON 98195

Department of Mathematics

2/29/88

To: Registrar

From: ▓▓▓▓▓▓▓▓▓▓, *Professor of Mathematics*

Re. Chukwubike Nworjih

Mr. Nworjih was a student in my history of Math class (420) in Summer quarter 1987. He completed all of the work including the final exam and earned a grade of 2.7 in this course. That is the grade that he should have received.

UNIVERSITY OF WASHINGTON
SEATTLE, WASHINGTON 98195

Department of Mathematics

29 February 1988

Registrar
University of Washington

This is to certify that Mr. Chukwubike Nworjih attended my course Math 407A in the Winter Quarter 1987 and faithfully completed all the work. The grade due him for this work was 2.7.

▓▓▓▓▓▓▓▓

Prof. of Mathematics

Mr. Chukwubike Nworgh
(xxxx615)
took the exams in Economics 201
in the Winter Quarter 1987,
and I have a grade for him
in the course.

███████████████

5#3-xxxx

DK-30

Harbour Homes™

by Geonerco, Inc.

1914 N. 34th St., Suite ~~101~~ 302 / Seattle, WA 98103   (206) 547-8213

3/22/88

To whom it may concern:

Mr Chukwubike Nworjih attended and completed math 303 V at the University of Washington during winter quarter, 1987. His official status in that class was never clear to me throughout the quarter. However, he did not appear on the computerized grade sheet which I submitted at the end of the quarter. I believe I submitted a class record to Sandra Murray in the mathematics Dept on which I recorded a final grade for Mr. Chukwubike Nworjih. If this grade is not available I can use his midterm and final exams which I have in my possession to work up a course grade for him.

Sincerely,

███████████

Instructor, MATH 303 V
Winter quarter 1987
547-xxxx or 782-xxxx

I was very grateful for all the time and efforts that Mr. Frank Byrdwell Jr. devoted to my problems, and helped me to register those courses, once I received the signed written letters from the six Professors from whom I took those courses. Mr. Frank Byrdwell Jr. personally took the letters from me, and on my behalf, went and talked to Mr. W. W. (Tim) Washburn, who was the Executive Director of Admission and Records.

Mr. Washburn called me into his office to ascertain exactly what happened. I explained to him in details, how I took those courses without paying my tuition fees, because I was on welfare, and I did not have the money to pay for the courses. I told him that the Professors had given me signed written letters that stated what courses I took, and the grades given to me for those courses.

Mr. Washburn and Mr. Frank Byrdwell Jr. read the letter that I wrote to the school authority, in which I pleaded for them to allow me to officially register the courses that I took in the 1987 academic year. I also wrote in that letter what I did, how I went to school without official registration in those classes, which was illegal according to the school policies. I told Mr. Washburn that what I did was the only way I could help myself, and get out of the welfare situation in which I found myself at that period of my life.

After I told my story to Mr. Washburn, he wrote an approval letter for me to pay and register for those courses with their grades. Here is the copy of the letter given to me by Mr. Washburn to register and pay for my courses.

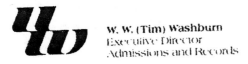

W. W. (Tim) Washburn
Executive Director
Admissions and Records

3/15/88

Frank Byrdwell

Frank —

This is most unusual but
I am approving the attached
registrations for Mrs. Chukwubike
xxxx615 —

He will have to pay the
late reg. fee for each qtr
as indicated on the attached
yellow sheet. The tuition
amount for WTR 87 may
be too high — I didn't have
the 86-87 schedule. Thank you.

Tim Washburn

University of Washington
320 Schmitz Hall, PC–30
Seattle, Washington 98195
(206) 543–5537

3/15/88

I was very happy and grateful that both of them helped me to register for those courses, because if I had not registered the courses, it would have taken me another year or two to graduate. After I had officially registered and added those twenty two course credits and their grades to my transcripts, I had five course credits short of graduation, because one hundred and eighty (180) credits were needed to graduate. Since I had started working at that time, I took a course in Basic Statistics, which was for five course credits at the distance learning class of the University of Washington Extension School, which was a branch of the University of Washington. I finished the course just in time to graduate with a Bachelor of Arts degree in Mathematics in December 15, 1988.

My education achievement was lower than my expectations in terms of my Grade Point Average score and the degree I received, because I planned to get a Bachelor of Science degree in Mathematics, but ended up with a Bachelor of Art degree. At that period of my life, all I wanted to do was to graduate and get out of school, because I was burnt out. My graduation with a Bachelor of Arts degree in Mathematics, proved that if someone sets their mind on a particular goal and strive as much as possible towards achieving that goal, they could achieve it, no matter the obstacles and the number of years it might take to achieve that goal.

Five years after my graduation, I had the urge to acquire more knowledge and education especially in computer fields. Therefore, in 1993, I received a Diploma degree in COBOL programming and also a Diploma in Web Design from a Correspondence School. Though I had the aspiration to study for a master's and doctorate degrees, but after what I went through, just to get my undergraduate degree, coupled with all the discriminations I had at my jobs, I was not mentally ready for any more schooling.

The Jobs that I deed

I must have been the most unlucky person in this world regarding the bad experiences I had working for some companies. I do not know if I was ever destined to work for any company, both private and none private companies, because I had not been lucky working for either. For the three private companies and one government agency where I have worked for three years or more, I was discriminated against. I do not like to sue anybody, but when my rights were violated at random with disregard to the laws, I was left with no other option, so I sued the companies for discrimination.

How could someone work for four different companies, both private and government agency, and was discriminated against by all four companies. What a bad omen. That was my life in a nutshell. If any person had not been the subject of discrimination, they might not know the effects of discrimination. However, if you have been discriminated against, and you are a disabled black person, you would feel so rejected, lonely, sometimes depressed, emotionally stressful and mentally draining. Again, that was me, in a nutshell.

When I was discriminated against, especially on my jobs, I felt so rejected by the society, that sometimes I questioned my self worth. I said to myself, maybe I was not good enough in what I was doing, and that was the reason I was discriminated against. Sometimes I tried to reason, to find out if there was anything, I did that contributed to my being discriminated against, so that I could stop doing it. However, I could not find anything that I did wrong, except that I am a disabled black man.

Then when the same discrimination kept repeating itself from one company that I had worked to another company, I sometimes wonder, if I was even destined to work for people? The reason was that, I had not stayed and worked with any company for a long period without being discriminated against. Then I said to myself, do not quit, as long as I am still alive, I will keep striving to succeed in life until the day I die, though I am surviving against all odds.

When I came to the United States of America, I had in mind that I would have the opportunities to pursue and achieve whatever goals I set my mind to achieve. Boy was I wrong. Ever since I came to this country, I had one obstacle after another. Initially, when I started working, I did some odd jobs like Janitorial and dish washing jobs while going to school.

When I worked as a janitor in one of the offices in downtown Seattle, I would have been able to do the job if I was not a disabled person. The job would have been okay for paying my bills, but because of my handicap and the leg brace that I wear on my leg, it was very hard for me to stand up for a long period of time, dusting office desks, cleaning the restrooms and emptying garbage cans.

Janitorial job was hard on my leg, and I wanted to give it a trial to find out if I could really do it. However, the day my car was towed away after I finished working my evening shift, and wanted to go home and could not find my car, I quit that job. It happened that one day after I got off work at 9pm that night, and wanted to go home. I went to where I parked my car only to find out that it had been towed away. The reason was that I parked my car on a restricted meter that had the sign "Do not park from 6am to 9am and 3pm to 6pm" written on it. People were not supposed to park their cars on that meter during rush hours traffic from 6am to 9am and from 3pm to 6 pm. I parked at that meter with my handicap decal permit, with the thought that it was okay for me to park there. Obviously, my handicap decal permit was not enough, because my car was towed away.

When I did not find my car where I parked it, I thought that someone had stolen my car, because I was not familiar with the meter signs. One of the nearby store owners that saw when my car was towed, approached me and told me that my car was towed away, and he gave me the name of that towing company. I called my brother and told him what happened, and he told me that he would come and pick me up. I called the towing company from a pay phone and got all the information I needed in order to pick up my car. When my brother came and picked me up, we drove to the office of the towing company, I paid the towing fee and drove my car home.

From the time I found out that my car was towed, to the time I picked up my car, took me more than two hours. The money I paid to the towing company just to pick up my car was more than my week's pay as a Janitor. The only meters closer to the building where I worked, had those warning signs "Do not park from 6am to 9am and 3pm to 6pm" written on them. If I had decided to work in that area, my weekly wages would have been used to pay for the parking tickets and for towing my car, since my work hours were from 4pm to 9pm at night. That did not make any sense, because I would not have any money to spare after I paid those expenses. I put all those thoughts into consideration before I made the decision to quit the job. Therefore, my Janitorial job only lasted for one week.

A few days later, I got another job as a Dish Washer. I knew that dish washing job would be hard on my leg, because it required a lot of standing, and there was the possibility that I might slip and fall on a wet floor. However, I needed the money to pay for my rent and school fees, so I had to do it. As one could imagine, the floor was always wet while washing the dishes. One day as I walked across the wet floor, I slipped, but caught my balance as I held on to one of the big trays where we stack dry dishes. After that incident, all I said to myself, was that I would never come back there once I clocked out for the day. That was exactly what I did, because I quit that job the next day. Therefore, my dish washing job only lasted for three days.

How the nightmare of my adventurous job experiences began

MY JOB AT AN INDUSTRIAL LAUNDRY COMPANY

A few weeks after quitting my job as a Dish washer, I got a job as a Soil Sorter with an Industrial Laundry Company in November 1980. It was a laundry company for different hospitals in Seattle, and it had different stages of operations. When dirty linens from the hospitals are collected and returned to the laundry facilities, they go through six stages. The first three stages are called "Soiled departments", since they occurred before the linens were washed. In these departments, linens are retrieved, sorted and washed. The last three stages are called "Clean departments", since they involved clean linens. In these departments, the linens are processed, packaged and distributed.

In the soil departments, the linens are contaminated with bloodstains, and have all kinds of human wastes you could imagine, before they are retrieved, sorted and washed. For standard safety precautions, the workers in these departments are required to use personal protective gears like surgery masks on their faces, surgery gowns and gloves on their hands.

I worked in the soil departments of the company, and my work hours were from 4pm to 10pm and sometimes 11pm at night. I normally go to school in the morning from 7am to 3pm. Once I got off school, I drove to a fast food restaurant, bought some foods and ate in the car while I drove to work. The job was a manual work, because we sorted and separated the dirty hospital linens and had them ready for the washing machines.

It required a lot of standing and it was very hard on my legs. When I stood up for a long time with my leg brace on, my legs were swollen and it hurt a lot at night when I came home. To minimize the pain in my legs, what I normally do was to take the leg brace off my leg in the restroom of the company, because I could walk without my leg brace. I only wear the leg brace, because it gives me much stability while walking, and to prevent me from falling if I step on stones.

I did not like the job, but it was better and paid more than what I earned as a Janitor or as a Dish Washer. I worked in the company just to pay my rent and my school fees. Sometimes when I got off work, I was so tired that I fell asleep while eating. I woke up around 4am in the morning to do my homework assignments before going to school at 7am. It was very difficult doing that kind of job and going to school. Sometimes my grades at school were lower than expected, because I did not study hard enough.

After about one year and seven months on the job, I was offered the job of a supervisor in the soil department, because of my dedication and hard work. As a supervisor, I had to sit down while doing some of my duties in the office. It was much easier on my legs and I did not take my leg brace off. I stood up sometimes and supervised other workers on the floor.

Some of my coworkers were jealous of me, because most of them have been with the company for more than five to six years and were not given the opportunity to be a supervisor. However, here I was, after one year and seven months on the job, I became a supervisor. We have many Nigerians that worked in that Industrial laundry company, because of the work hours. It allowed many of us students to go to school in the morning, and then after school, we went to work in the evening from 4pm to 10pm and sometimes 11pm. Since I became a supervisor, some of my Nigerian coworkers were unhappy and stubborn, to the point that they made my job difficult, and were not cooperative sometimes when they were told what to do. They deed certain things that did not comply with the policy of the company.

As the supervisor of the soil department, I made sure that we maintained a constant workflow to the other sections of the plants. The works were physical in nature because one had to stand up during the whole duration of the shift, sorting and separating the linens into different carts with the same linens. Though it was tiring, but we did take 10 minutes break every two hours, so that the workers could keep up with the workflows.

Linda was a black American female that worked in the morning shift of the soil department. She was the girlfriend of Jackson, my former supervisor. Jackson used to supervise the night shift soil department from 4pm to 10pm. When there was an opening in the morning shift of the soil department from 7am to 4pm, the company gave Jackson the supervisor job for that shift, and I was the supervisor in the evening shift from 4pm to 10pm and sometimes 11pm.

When Linda started working in the morning shift of the soil department, Jackson was her supervisor. As days passed by, Linda and Jackson developed interest with each other and later became boyfriend and girlfriend. Sometimes Linda came to work late and would not get a verbal or a written warning from Jackson, since she was his girlfriend. But if the other coworkers that worked with Linda came to work late, they received a written warning. Many of her coworkers complained that Jackson was playing favoritism with Linda. During one of the management meetings, they decided that since Jackson and Linda were in a relationship, that they would not work in the same department, just to avoid conflict of interest. Therefore, Linda was transferred to the evening shift that started at 4pm until closing. That was how Linda ended up in my shift.

Linda was not as fast as the other male coworkers that worked on the conveyor belt. Therefore, to maintain the constant rate of speed of the conveyor belt, she worked at the end of the belt where there were no bedspreads and other large linens to pull. Her co-workers construe that to imply that I was doing her a favor, since they were all paid equally. They argued that since they have the same job title and were paid the same amount of money, that she supposed to do the same kind of work that they do, and work on different areas of the conveyor belt.

Sometimes some of the Nigerian coworkers deliberately slowed down the conveyor belt where the dirty linens were sorted. When that happened, and we did not produce the number of pounds required each hour in order to keep the workflow to the other sections of the plants adequately, the supervisor takes the blame for lack of coordination and planning of the departments.

As the relationship between Linda and Jackson got serious, Linda decided to move in and lived with Jackson. When we got off work, Jackson normally picked her up and both of them drove home. Linda was always known to be happy and bubbly, but some days she came to work looking so sad and unhappy. When I asked her why she looked so sad, she told me that she argued all the time with Jackson, and that he slapped her during one of those arguments. As the days passed by, she became so distant and did not like to sit and eat with other coworkers in the lunchroom during lunch hours or chat with anybody. When I asked her why she became withdrawn, she told me that Jackson threatened her not to discuss what happened between them with anybody.

There were certain days when Linda came to work and her face and other parts of her bodies were bruised. Those bruises were the result of the beaten, she received from her boyfriend Jackson. On many occasions, I asked her how she got those bruises. She just gave me a verge excuse and refused to tell me. One day she came to work and one of her eyes was so bruised and swollen that she could not open the eye. When I asked her what happened to her eye, for the first time, she opened up and told me that it was from the beaten she received from her boyfriend Jackson. She said that she wanted to tell me what happened to her, because she was scared that her boyfriend might kill her one day and nobody would know what happened to her. She told me that the severity of the beaten was too much for her, because her boyfriend Jackson used Television cable wire to beat her up, and that she thought that she would not survive that night.

She told me that sometimes when she did not have the urge of having sex with him, because of the pains she had from the beaten, her boyfriend would have sex with her anyway regardless of the pain she had. She told me how her boyfriend kept having sex with her when her vagina was bruised and bleeding, and she begged him to stop, but he did not listen to her and her vagina was badly bruised, and she was unable to walk. She told me that the few days she did not come to work was because of the bruises she had on her vagina that prevented her from walking.

After she told me all those horrible stories, she asked me if I could do her a favor. I asked her what kind of favor was that. She told me that she was afraid that one day, Jackson her boyfriend would kill her and no one would know how she died. She asked me if I would give her a ride home when we got off work, to one of her girlfriends house. I told her yes. The reason she asked me for a ride was because they lived a few blocks away from the company, and her boyfriend normally came and gave her a ride home.

I told her that all she had to do was to get into my car when we got off work, and I would drop her off where ever she wanted. I knew that I took a big risk when I interfered in her personal life with her boyfriend, because both of them were my coworkers, and her boyfriend was a supervisor. However, sometimes, someone had to take some risk in life in order to save someone else life, and that was exactly what I did.

It was an awkward scene the first day that I gave Linda a ride. When we got off work, her boyfriend had already parked his car and was waiting for her to come and get in, so that both of them would drive home together. Instead, he saw his girlfriend Linda, followed me to my car. I opened the passenger door of my car for her, and she got in. Then I got into my car, started the engine and both of us drove off. Jackson her boyfriend honked at me, as if to say to me, what was going on, and what was I doing. I did not pay any attention to him as I drove away from the compound of the company. When he noticed that I was not going to stop, he followed us behind. As I was driving,

I knew that he was right behind me in his car, when I looked at my rear view mirror, but I did not know if he had a gun or not. However, my gut feeling was that I was going to help Linda regardless of what happened to me.

When I got to where she wanted me to drop her off, she opened the door and got out. I waited for her to go into her girlfriend's house before I left. Her boyfriend parked a little distance from where I parked, and watched her got out of my car and went into her girlfriend's house. As I drove off, I wanted to know if her boyfriend was still following me, so I looked through the rear view mirror and noticed that his car was still parked there.

The following day we came to work, Linda's boyfriend Jackson, came to me just before he got off from his shift, and asked me why I gave his girlfriend a ride, and why did I interfered with their relationship? I told him that she asked me for a ride, so I gave her a ride. He told me not to give her a ride anymore, because I was interfering in their relationship. I told him that if she asked me for a ride, that I would give her a ride. Later that day, I told Linda that her boyfriend told me not to give her a ride anymore. She asked me if I would do what her boyfriend said. I told her no, and that if she wanted a ride, that I would give her a ride. She told me that she would need a ride when we got off work that day, and that she did not want to live with her boyfriend anymore. She said that she had wanted to move out of his house many times, but that he told her that if she moved out, that he would kill her.

I asked her how she would get her belongs from his house. She told me that he could have them, and that she would never go back to his house again. She said that she depended on me to give her a ride to her girlfriend's house when we got off work. For two weeks, her boyfriend came to give her a ride home after we got off work, but Linda refused to get into his car. After the third week, Jackson realized that Linda was serious about ending their relationship, and that she did not want to live with him any more. Therefore, he stopped coming to pick her up when we got off work. Since both of them still worked there, and Linda relied on me for emotional support and a ride home, other coworkers thought that I had taken her away from Jackson. Some of them asked me if we were boyfriend and girlfriend. I told them no, that we were not.

The broke up of Linda's relationship with Jackson, added to many chains of events within the company that lead to the termination of one Nigerian worker. This particular Nigerian worker by the name Paul, was determined to make my job very difficult. He refused to comply with certain policies of the company, and deliberately came to work late, and bragged that I would not do anything to him. Part of my job as a supervisor was to make sure that we maintain a constant workflow to the other sections of the company. Sometimes when I saw that someone deliberately slowed down the conveyor belt with all the dirty linens, I asked that individual to release the belt in order to speed up production.

It happened that one day Paul was sorting dirty linens and he deliberately slowed down the belt. I told him to release the belt, so that other workers could help with the sorting of the linens. He refused and became very angry. He asked me why I did not tell Linda to pull the sheets, which was a little harder to sort. He cursed me out by using different profanity languages, and said some derogatory statements to me.

The laundry company was built in such a way that each department depends on the other departments for their production output. The

Soil department, which was my department, sets the pace of the workflow to the other departments of the company. Therefore, if my department did not work fast enough to produce the work of the other departments, then there would be total workflow slowdown in the company. It was the responsibility of the supervisor to make sure that we maintained a constant workflow. However, sometimes some of those jealous Nigerian workers purposely slowed down the pace of work, only to have me take the blame for it, since I was the supervisor.

Paul was one Nigerian employee that was very stubborn and disobedient in whatever he was told to do. He later accused me of giving preferential treatment to Linda, because he alleged that she was my girlfriend. Linda was never my girlfriend, and I have explained the incident about Linda and Jackson, and how I got myself involved in their relationship, because she asked me for a ride when we got off work, so some of my coworkers assumed that she was my girlfriend.

Paul had a nonchalant attitude towards work in general, because he used to come to work late most of the time. He disliked me, and did not respect my opinion on whatever project we did. In one of the company meetings, he showed how disrespectful he was to me, when I was asked for my opinions in the discussions we had. He was agitated and angry that I was asked for my opinion. His attitude got so bad that I bought a logbook, or rather a diary and started writing down certain events of the day in the book. Some of what I wrote in the diary was as follows.

At the meeting we had on 8/4/1982, all the night shift employees were told that once the bell rang, that everyone would report to their different work assignments. They were told that whoever was ten minutes late to work, would be giving a writing warning. Paul was among those present in the meeting, and he was the only one that stood up and gave me a warning. He said that if I threaten him, that he would beat me up.

On 8/7/1982, Paul left the conveyor belt at 3:16pm and did not come back until we got off work. On 8/14/1982, John, who was another Nigerian worker left the conveyor belt at 3:12pm, after he told me that he was sick, and did not come back to work until the closing hour.

On 8/15/1982, Paul came to work and clocked in at 6:37am. He drove off with his car and then came back at 7:15am. That same day John was late for work and clocked in at 7:17am. I wrote those comments in my logbook that morning, but the incident that happened later that day was the one that got Paul terminated.

Twenty minutes after we started work that morning of 8/15/1982, I noticed that we did not have enough people to work on the conveyor belt, so I had to inform the Production Manager about the situation. Any time I step away from the office, I normally close the office door, but on that particular day, I left the office door open and went downstairs, and talked to the Production Manager. I asked him if I could call some people to come and work on the conveyor belt, since we were short staffed that day. After I made those calls, I came upstairs and went into the office, and I noticed that someone came into the office and tore off the pages of what I wrote about Paul from my logbook.

I wanted to know the number of people that went into my office while I was gone. So I called John and asked him if he went into my office while I was gone. He said no at first, but when he saw that I was serious about the question, he said yes. He told me that Paul went into my office and read what I wrote about him in my logbook, and while he was on the conveyor belt, Paul called him to come and read what I wrote about them in my logbook. He said that after he read it, that he went back to the conveyor belt while Paul was still in my office, and that he did not see who tore off the pages from my logbook.

I called Paul and asked him if he entered my office while I was gone. He said yes. I asked him if he tore out the pages of what I wrote about him from my logbook, after reading it. He said no. I knew he was the one that did it, because only three people went into the office when I was gone. The third person was the soil linen dumper, and he was authorized to go into the office if I was there or not. He went into the office and printed some figures from the computer.

I took the time card of Paul to the Production Manager, and explained to him what happened that morning. I told him that I came to work at 6:20am and was there when Paul came to work and clocked in at 6:37am. I saw when he drove off with his car to drop off his girlfriend and then came back to work at 7:15am. I did not say anything to him when he came back. What I did was that I wrote the incident that happened that morning in my logbook. Then when I came upstairs after I made some phone calls, I saw him in the hallway and told him that next time, that he should clock in five or ten minutes before the hour that he was to start work, in order to avoid what happened that morning.

The Production Manager told me to tell Paul to come to his office, which was downstairs. After a while, Paul came upstairs and said all sorts of derogatory things to me. I did not respond to whatever he said. The Production Manager came upstairs a few minutes later and called John into my office. He asked him if he saw the person that tore the pages out of my logbook. John said no. He told him to go back to the conveyor belt. The Production Manager told me that the following day, that he would discuss the whole incident of what happened with Jackson, who was the day shift supervisor, and he went back to his office.

I went to the conveyor belt and supervised how the workflow was going. As soon as Paul saw me, he rushed to where I was on the belt and threatened to beat me up. However, John, another Nigerian who was working on the conveyor belt, held him back. Paul said that he would harm me, and that he would slap the glasses on my face right into my eyes. I left the conveyor belt and went to my office. I picked up the phone and told the Production Manager what happened after he saw Paul.

The Production Manager came upstairs and asked the people on the conveyor belt if Paul threatened to beat me up. They told him yes, and the Production Manager told Paul to go home. I thought that the Production Manager told him to go home for that day, so that things would calm down, since he had already told me that he would discuss the whole incident with Jackson the following day. I later found out that when the Production Manager told Paul to go home, that what he really meant, was that he was terminated.

Paul refused to leave the building, and did not obey the Production Manager. He went back to the conveyor belt and kept arguing with the Production Manager, and told him that he would fight back. As the Production Manager went to my office and picked up the phone to call the police, Paul left the building and went home. I was so frightened about the whole incident, that I later called the police and reported what Paul said to me, that he would beat me up and harm me.

After Paul was terminated, he later sued the company, and cited that he was not given adequate warning before he was terminated. The company policy stated that someone should be given a written warning first, before termination. Since the company did not want to drag the whole incident in the court, they paid him some money and settled his case out of court.

During the period when all these incidents happened, the company changed management and a new General Manager was hired to run the company. He had a military background on his resume, and during his introduction speech, he told us that there would be some reduction in workforce, as the company was trying to reorganize under a new management. After a few weeks on the job, the General Manager reshuffled some of the supervisors to different duties and to other departments. In my case, he gave me the job of a Leadman for the second shift soil department, which was a step lower than my previous job as a supervisor. He stated that the reason I was given the job of the Leadman, was because of reduction in work force.

The General Manager knew that I was a disabled person, and that I wore a leg brace on my right leg, because during one of the staff meetings we had, he asked me what happened to my leg, and I told him that I had polio when I was a child. I would have taken the job of the Leadman without objection, however, what worried me the most was the job descriptions and the duties of the Leadman in the second shift soil department. Because it was much different from the duties of the Leadman in the first shift of the soil department, and both Leads workers are in the same department.

When Paul was terminated after the incident he had with me, the company paid him some money and settle his lawsuit out of court. The new General Manager wanted me to leave the company, but he did not know how to accomplish that without violating the civil right act law. The only option he had was that he gave me a difficult task to do, so that if I could not do it, then I would quit on my own initiative or accord. The job descriptions of the Leadman stated that I had to unload the linen carts that weighed 500 to 700 pounds from the trucks, and then do other tasks, which I considered strenuous on my leg. When the General Manager gave me the job descriptions of the Leadman, I told him that I could not do the job, but he told me to do the job, quit or be terminated. I decided to do the job instead of quitting. After I did that job for a few days, I was injured, and was not able to do the job any more. I collected workers compensation benefits for about two years for my injury.

I filed a disability discrimination complaint against the company with Washington State Human Right Office in August 1983. An investigator was assigned to investigate my case. A few days after she took my case, she had a biased mind, and took sides with the company. She harassed me, and told me to withdraw my case. I filed a complaint with the supervisor of the investigator. Her supervisor did not believe some of the allegations I wrote in my complaint about the investigator. So in order to prove that the investigator threatened me, I took a hiding tape recorder to one of the interviews I had with the investigator. After I made that tape, I had an appointment with her supervisor. In that meeting, I played the recorded tape of how the investigator threatened me to withdraw my case.

On the tape, the investigator stated how she would ruin my case, because the company told her that I was not authorized to work in this country. She threatened me to withdraw my case or she would enter a no fault finding on the part of the company. What the company and the investigator did not know, was that I was already a Permanent Resident of the United State of America, and I had a green card, which legally authorized me to work in this country.

Her supervisor told me that regardless of my work status, that the investigator would have been neutral in her judgment. Another investigator was appointed to take over the investigation of my case. However, I felt that my case was delayed unnecessarily due to the biased attitude of the investigators. In May 1985, the agency gave me the right to sue letter and closed my case.

I filed a disability discrimination lawsuit against the company in the Superior Court of the State of Washington for King County in March 19, 1986, Case number 84–2–18060–9, and the trial date for the lawsuit was set for July 21, 1986.

After one year of legal maneuvers and depositions, the company found out that I was a legal Permanent resident, and was authorized to work in the United State of America. They decided to settle my case three days before the court hearing on July 18, 1986. However, I won some monetary settlement in my case, but it was a painful experience to go through discrimination. They offered me another job in the company, I said no, because I wanted to move on with my life, and did not want to go back and work at that company.

When I was injured on my job at Industrial Laundry Company, the doctor gave me some medication pills for my pains. I also received some therapy treatments twice a week. During the period of my treatment, I tried to commit suicide, which I did intentionally, because I needed some help, and wanted to highlight the injustices that I had in my company. I would never commit suicide, no matter how bad my situation might be or how stressful the condition. Suicide does not run in our family and I would not be the first person to do that.

The so called suicide was a planned one, which I did in a way not to harm myself in the process. It was a cry for help. This was how the suicide incident happened. When I was injured, I had pains in my back, neck and leg. I was given some valium pills that I took three times a day for pains. I also saw a therapist in the hospital for my back pains. One morning before I went to the hospital for my appointment to see the therapist, I took one pill of valium. These pills were supposed to be taken three times a day at eight hour intervals. I also took the bottle of the prescription with me to the hospital. When I arrived at the hospital, I went into the therapy room and the nurse had me lay down on the bed for treatment.

At one point during my treatment, the nurse left the room, went and saw another patient. At that time, I was almost sleepy, because of the one valium pill I took before I came to the hospital. When I saw the nurse coming into the room, I brought out the bottle of valium from my pocket, opened it and put two more valiums pills into my mouth. Therefore, the total number of valium pills I took was three, which was the number of pills prescribed for me to take for the day. When the nurse was almost in the room, and I knew she would see whatever I did, I poured the whole valium of pills on my hand as if I wanted to take all of them. The nurse held my hand, and at that point, I was almost sleepy, but heard all the conversations. The nurse called for help and I was taken to the emergency room, where some of the valium pills in my body were pumped out of my bloodstream.

When I recovered and was discharged from the hospital, I was treated for stress and depression for a while. Then I moved on, tried and rebuilt my life after I settled my discrimination lawsuit with the Industrial Laundry Company. The discrimination experiences made me stronger, wiser and strengthen my faith in God, and gave me the will power to fight back whenever I noticed any signs of discrimination directed towards me. Anyway, I picked up the pieces and moved on with my life.

My job at the Bank

Before I graduated from the University of Washington, I applied and got an entry level job as an Accounting Specialist with a Bank. I thought that all the discrimination issues that I had were behind me, since I was starting with a new company and with a new prospect in life, and hoped that I would be given an opportunity for advancement in the bank. Boy was I wrong.

The bank turned out to be one of the worst discriminatory institutions I had ever come across and worked for in my life. I worked for more than three years in an entry level position with the bank, and the only change I had within those years was the eighty cent salary increase I received.

I applied for more than fifty internal job openings and did not get any of the jobs, because the personnel department told me that I did not have the minimum qualifications for the jobs. However, those jobs were given to other people with less minimum qualifications than I do. Remember, I have a degree in Mathematics and was not given the opportunity to contribute my talent and skills to that banking institution.

In the Funds Transfer Department of the bank where I worked, I applied for more than twenty job openings, but was not hired for any of the jobs. The jobs were given to some people who did not apply for the jobs or have less experience than I do, but were hired and trained to do the jobs, simply because they were white employees. When I complained to the management of the department and to some personnel officials, a nonchalant attitude was given to my complaint. Nothing was done to resolve my problems. All they did was referred me from one official to another, only to come up with the same negative result.

Let me detail same pattern of racial discrimination in Funds Transfer Department of the bank. I applied for a job opening in the Funds Transfer Department and was interviewed by the supervisor. Later she told me that she gave the job to a white female who was then the customer service supervisor. However, that was not true, because the job was given to a white male who did not even applied for the job. He worked in the customer service section, but was trained to do the job. I told the Vice President of the department about the incident, and he told me that the supervisor had the right to give the job to whomever she preferred.

I applied for the job opening in the Home Equity Loans department, but was not given the job. Instead, it was given to another white employee who had less qualification than I do. She was trained for the job, and after the training, she was not able to do the job. She left the bank job instead of making mockery of herself.

I applied for another job opening in Funds Transfer Department, and was interviewed by the supervisor. Later she told me that she gave the job to another male employee, and the reason she did not give me the job was my accent. I told the Vice President about the reasons the supervisor gave for not hiring me for the job. He told me that the supervisor had the right to choose whomever she wanted. This white male that got the job, was first hired in the customer service section of the Funds Transfer Department, and within seven months, he got another job in the Remittance section. Then, within a few months again, he was working in the control section as a System Specialist. All those changes to the new jobs, had salary increases. But for me who had worked for more than three years in the department was still on my first job.

On many occasions, I complained to the Vice President of our department, that I applied for many internal job openings, but was not hired for any of the jobs. I also told him, how one particular supervisor on three occasions denied me job opportunity, and in one job interview, she used some racial excuses for not hiring me. Still nothing was done to correct the situation.

After some months and nobody investigated my complaint, I wrote a letter to the Board members. Then I went and talked to Vice President of the Personnel department, and told her that I was about to mail the letter to some board members of the bank. She advised me not to send the letters out as I intended. Anyway, she referred me to the Employee Relations Specialist, who I had met before, but he did not help me.

The day I met the Employee Relations Specialist again, to discuss my problems, he did not like the idea that I wrote the letter addressed to the Board members. He told me that he would set up an appointment for me to talk to the Senior Employment Consultant. The day I met and talked to the Senior Employment Consultant, she told me that she had nothing much she could do to help me, since the supervisors made the ultimate decisions on whomever they hired. She advised me to take some career courses, which I informed her that I had already taken. She said that it would improve my chances of getting a job within the bank. That was the first and last time I talked to her.

I waited for about two years and my problems got worse. I was tired of been referred from one official to another with no relief in sight. Therefore, I went and filed a complaint with the Equal Employment Opportunity Commission (EEOC) in October 10, 1990. However, I withdrew the charges when the Vice President of the department promised me that he would resolve my problems. He said that I would be considered for any job opening that I applied for within the department.

Then when we had two job openings in our department, the Vice President interviewed me for one of the job openings, and I was interviewed for the other job opening by the supervisor who had refused to hire me on more than three occasions. After those interviews, and I was not hired for any of the job openings, that was when I realized that the Vice President was not serious in solving my problems. On February 26, 1991, I went to the Equal Employment Opportunity Commission and refilled my charges of discrimination against the bank.

In Funds transfer department where I worked, the supervisor and the Vice President used Janet, one of the white female employee, who was a bully, to do their dirty works for them. Janet would say certain comments to someone just to provoke that person to the point that they would say nasty things back to her. Then, if the employee made some stupid comments, and used some profanity words that might be contrary to the company's policies, she would report that individual to the supervisor and the Vice President, and that employee was given a written warning or terminated.

The supervisor and the Vice President pretended as if they did not know what Janet was doing. However, they encouraged her to do her devious deeds, only to use that to write people up. In fact, any time the supervisor and the Vice President wanted to terminate someone in the department, they would transfer that employee to Janet's section of the department.

One of the bank policy stated, that if an employee had more than five errors within a month, that employee would be terminated. So what happened was that, any employee that was targeted for termination, was transferred to Janet's section, because of her devious ways of dealing with people. She made sure that the employee that was targeted for termination accumulated that many errors in their personal file. Then the employee was given the option to quit or was terminated.

When I was transferred to Janet's section, I did not apply to work there. The supervisor told me that the Vice President wanted me to work in that section, because they wanted me to convince them that I could work and cooperate with my coworkers. I wondered what he meant by that, or maybe it was a set up, to see if I could work with Janet, because we knew her reputation for being a bully. They thought that they would get me in their trap and had me terminated. Anyway, what I suspected happened one day, when I went and asked one of my coworkers within that section a question. Janet stood up, and told my coworker not to answer my question. She told me to go back to my site, because they were too busy for any question.

In fact, Janet talked to me as if I was her little child. I said to myself, that this must be a set up. I went to the Vice President and told him how rudely Janet talked to me. I told him that if he transferred me to work with Janet, so that she would give me a hard time, that it would never work. I asked him if it was a set up, when he told me to go and work in that section. He said no. I told him that I would take a legal action, if they used Janet to provoke me, and then use that to write me up or terminate me. The fact was that, I beat them to their own games, because everything they did to upset me, backfired on them. I exposed what Janet deed to me, and to other employees to the Vice President. The Vice President later cautioned Janet, and told her that I was too smart, and that she was not dealing with a fool.

Another incident of discrimination happened one day when some employees were making jokes about what they saw on Television regarding Acquired immune deficiency (AIDS). Someone said that what they saw on Television, showed that AIDS originated from Africa. Janet said no, that AIDS was from Nigeria, and that she saw some monkeys in that program that was shown on Television. The supervisor and some of the employees around there were laughing, when the Vice President of the department walked by. He asked them why they were laughing. They told him that it was about the program they saw on Television regarding AIDS and Africa. The Vice President told them to ask me. He said that, because they knew that I was originally from Nigeria. The reason why the Vice President of the department, wanted them to ask me about racial remarks was beyond me.

More incident of racial discrimination happened one day, when I came back from break and stood by my desk. Janet told me to sit down, and go into the queue on the computer and process some projects for her. I told her not to talk to me as if I was her child. She got mad, and said you Nigeria motherfucker, do what I told you to do. I went and told the supervisor about the incident, and the profanity language that Janet used towards me. But the supervisor told me not to talk to his Lead in that manner, and that I should go and sit down. The reason why he did not take any action about the name calling, was that he himself had called me Nigerian motherfucker. That incident happened when the Vice President came by his cubicle and inquired about the project I was doing. The supervisor was annoyed, and told him that the Nigeria motherfucker had low output productions. He knew that I overheard what he said, but he told the Vice President, that he did not care if I overheard what he said.

There was another discriminatory remark, made by my supervisor during one of my conversations with him and the Vice President of our department. That happened in the conference room, when the Vice President and my supervisor told me that I delayed some of the projects I was doing for about an hour. They told me that I would be given a written warning, if it happened again. As I was leaving the conference room, my supervisor said, that this Nigger thought that he could do anything he wanted and get away with it.

The discrimination in that bank was so obvious and too demoralizing, that I wrote a letter to the board members of the bank and explained my problems and frustrations. When I showed the letter to the Vice President of the personnel department, she advised me not to send the letter to the board members, and that they would investigate the matter. Ten months after I wrote that letter, nothing changed, and I did not get another job within the bank. I told the Vice President of my department and the personnel department, that I would take a legal action against the bank. They ignored me.

Sometimes during the days, I had terrible headaches, just because I was working in a hostile and stressful work environment, where discrimination was pervasive and nobody wanted to help me, because the management had a nonchalant attitude towards my situation. Though the environment was very stressful, but I did not want to quit the job on my own, because I knew that if I quit on my own, I would not be able to collect unemployment benefit. I was frustrated, and since I could not get any remedy from the bank regarding my problems, I went to the Equal Employment Opportunity Commission (EEOC) and filed a complaint for discrimination. A few days after the bank received the copy of the discrimination complaint from EEOC, I was terminated from my job.

I relied on the EEOC for justice on my case, and it took them some time to finish the investigation of my complaint. When they gave me the right to sue letter, I took the bank to court. In March 3, 1992, I file a lawsuit against the company for discrimination in the Superior Court of the State of Washington, Case number 92-2-05177- 0, and the trial date was set for October 14, 1993. A few months after I filled the lawsuit in court, the bank finally agreed to settle the case out of court, after they saw the overwhelming evidence of discrimination I had against the company.

During the settlement negotiation, the company paid me some money, and also offered me another job within the bank. I told them no, because I wanted to get out of that environment and moved on with my life. The bank later terminated my supervisor and the Vice President of that department where I worked.

After I left my job at the Bank, I spent a couple of months looking for another job without any success. A friend of mine, who was the President of the company in charge of many of the Hospital Laundry companies in the United State of America, offered me the job of a Production supervisor in one of their branches in Lansing Michigan. The job was similar to the job I had at the Industrial Laundry Company in the 1980's, which was the laundry company for some hospitals in Seattle. Some of the dirty hospital linens had bloodstains, and I do not like seeing bloods. However, I had many bills to pay, and when I did not have the money to pay for all those bills, I took whenever job I could get.

His company paid all the expenses to ship my properties and my car to Michigan. So in March 1993, I packed my belongings and moved to Lansing Michigan. Moving to Michigan was an adventure on itself to me, because Michigan was famous for its snow during winter. I did not know that before I moved over there.

I like working in an environment where there are different race of people, but I noticed, that the majority of the people that worked in that company were black, and most of them are relatives or friends of the Director. The Director of the company was a black man, and he hired most of his relatives or friends to work in that company. As the Production Supervisor, I like to get along with my coworkers, and I do not like to discipline people without adequate thought and warning.

I also noticed that some of the relatives and friends of the Director came to work late, and some of them disobeyed him when he told them to do certain things. They looked down on him as if to say, you are my relative and friend, so why do you want me to work too hard. It was very difficult to run a company that way.

What happened was that, any time the Director wanted to discipline any of those employees, he instructed me to do it for him. There was an incident when the Director wanted to terminate one of his relatives, and I was not aware of any particular wrong the relative committed, but he instructed me to tell his relative that he was terminated. I asked him what was the reason for the termination. He told me just to tell his relative that he was terminated. I told the Director, that since I did not have enough reason to terminate him, that I was uncomfortable telling his relative that he was terminated. I did not know if they had some argument at home, or what really happened, that he wanted to terminate his relative. I did not like to terminate employees without adequate reasons, so I quit the job, after working there for about a year.

I was very grateful that my friend gave me the job opportunity in Michigan, but if I had known then, that it snowed a lot during winter over there, I would never have gone there to live. During the winter period that I lived in that state, I stayed home most of the time, and only went to work when the roads were cleared of snow, for me to walk and drive my car. Anyway, after the storm and snowy winter of 1993, I waited until the winter was over, and then I moved back to

Seattle in the early part of March 1994.

MY JOB AT A FREIGHT COMPANY

A few months after I moved back to Seattle, I got a temporary job with a Freight company. The work I did was not challenging to my skills, but the income that I received paid my bills. I just stayed with the company and did my best, with the hope that one day things would get better. One year later, I became a permanent employee with the company, and hoped that I would be given the opportunity to progress and built a career in the company. However, it turned out to be one of the worst companies, where discrimination occurred at random. Then I asked myself, what have I done wrong, or was it just bad luck on my part, that I end up working with discriminatory companies. I spent four precious years of my life working for the Freight Company, and did not achieve anything. These are some of the discrimination experiences I had when I worked at the Freight Company.

Randy was one of the managers at the Human Resource Department of the Freight Company that used my race, national origin and my disability to discriminate against me, and denied me interview with the hiring supervisors. This manager took it upon himself, that as long as he was the Employment Representative who had to review my applications first, before he referred me to the hiring supervisors, that I did not stand the chance in getting any job with the company. He discriminated against me with impunity, and had a nonchalant attitude towards my complaints. His behavior manifested itself, whenever I went to his office for an interview, or when he called and told me that he would not refer me to the hiring supervisors for further interviews.

I applied for more than thirty job openings, in which Randy was the Employment Representative. Out of those job openings, only three of my application forms were forwarded to the hiring supervisors. He said that I did not meet the minimum requirements for the rest of the job openings, and for that reason, he did not forward my application forms to the hiring supervisors. Some of the employees that were hired in most of the job openings that I applied for, did not have the minimum qualification, but they were hired for the jobs.

Randy told some of the supervisors and Directors that I was originally from Nigeria, but now a United States of America citizen. That was evident on the two interviews I had with two hiring supervisors. When I had an interview with one of those supervisors, he told me that Randy had told him that I was originally from Nigeria, and that he wanted to know a little bit of history about me. I did not ask him what the history he wanted to know about me was all about, since I was there for an interview. He asked me about the weather in Nigeria, and if we had two seasons or four in Nigeria. I told him that we have two seasons. He asked me how many languages we have in Nigeria, and how many of those languages that I spoke. I told him that we have many dialects, and that I spoke two languages. After some other discussion about the job, I left at the end of the interview. A few days later, Randy called and told me that the supervisor had given the job to another candidate.

In one incident, when I went to Randy's office for an interview for a job opening, he told me that he would not refer me to the hiring supervisor for further interview, because of my accent. His reason was that, the station staffs, the sales people and the vendors would find it difficult to understand my accent clearly, and that would lose some business for the company. After the interview, I told my supervisor about what Randy said, that the reason he did not refer me for an interview was because of my accent. She told me not to be discouraged by that comment, and to keep applying for any job openings that I felt that I could do, regardless of my accent, I thanked her and left.

During another job interview with Randy, he asked me again, where I came from originally. I told him that I believed that I had already told him many times before, that I was originally from Nigeria. He told me that he just wanted someone to remind him again, and refresh his memory that I was from Nigeria. A few days later, he called me and told me that he would not forward my application form for that job opening to the hiring supervisor.

I applied for a job opening in the Loss Control department. A few days later, the hiring supervisor interviewed me, and told me that I had nice working experience to do the job, and that my supervisor in the Claim department gave her a nice recommendation about me. She told me that I would be trained on what to do when given the job. Judging from the remarks and reaction of the supervisor during the interview, I thought that I would get the job, and that it was only a matter of days and I would start the new job.

When Randy heard that I applied for the job, and was interviewed by the supervisor, he told the supervisor and the Director of the department that I was originally from Nigeria, but now a United State of America citizen. I did not know what the information that I was originally from Nigeria had to do with my application for that job. Anyway, a few days later, Randy told me that the job was given to a different employee.

Another incident of how Randy influenced the decision of some of those hiring supervisors, happened when I had an interview with the supervisor for another job opening. In fact, that was one of the worst interviews I had in my life, because when I was in his office, I thought to myself, why did we discussed things that were irrelevant to the interview. How he knew so much about me, but I never met him before in my life. Once I stepped into his office, he said to me, I knew it, you are from Nigeria. I told him yes. He told me that Randy had told him a little bit of history about me. I said to myself, here we go again. The supervisor asked me if he pronounced my name correctly. I told him yes. He told me that he had a Nigerian teacher that taught his son mathematics, and that at first, he found it difficult to pronounce the teacher's name, but with practice, he was able to pronounce his name correctly. He told me that his son was studying for his second degree, and he asked me if I would study for a second degree. I told him that I had a diploma in COBOL programming, which I did not include in my resume. He asked me about the weather in Nigeria. I told him that compared to the temperatures we have here, it was warm over there. He told me that I spoke good English, and wrote well too based on my cover letter. I thanked him for those compliments.

He asked me if English was the second language of Nigerians. I told him yes. He asked me about the crime rate in Nigeria compared to what we have here in the United States of America. I asked him what kind of crime he was talking about. He told me violent crimes and other kinds of crimes. I told him that if someone stole some goods with any weapon, and they were caught, that they might be executed.

For other kinds of crimes, I told him that we had some corrupt Nigerians who could do anything to enrich themselves. He told me that they have that kind of people here in the United States of America too. He asked me how long I lived in Seattle. I told him about seventeen years in 1997, and that I went and lived in Michigan State for about a year when I got a job there. Then the supervisor switched to the duties and the description of the job. He talked about the expectation of the kind of person they wanted for the job. I told him that if given the opportunity, that I felt that I could do it to his satisfaction. At the end of the interview, I shook hands with him, thanked him and then left. A few weeks later, Randy called and told me that the job was given to someone else.

That kind of interview or rather interrogations I had with that supervisor, was the experiences I had with most of the supervisors that interviewed me for a job at the company. I did not do anything wrong to Randy to deserve the hostile and inhuman treatment I received from him. How he was determined, and made sure that I was not given any opportunity to progress, and contribute my talent to the company was beyond my wildest dream. Randy subjected me through some mental anguish, emotional stress, rejection, harassment and discrimination for more than two years. I reported him to the President of the personnel department, but nothing was done to remedy the situation.

Many times, I cried during my lunch break in the conference room, and then I asked God, when would the torture and suffering be over? Sometimes on my desk, tears would just drop down my eyes, because I was crying inside and asking for help, but I did not have anywhere to go for help in the company.

Only God knew the agony and pain of what rejection and discrimination had done in my life. Just for being a disabled black person, some members of the society subjected me from one discrimination after another. I had to prove myself in anything I did before I was accepted. All I asked for, was to be treated in a fair and just manner, and be given the opportunity to contribute my talent in whatever task, and show that I could be productive to the society. However, that opportunity was not given me to reach my potential in life.

The company had a nonchalant attitude towards my discrimination complaint, and how Randy hindered my progress within the company.

In April 1997, I filled a discrimination complaint against the Freight Company with the Equal Employment Opportunity Commission (EEOC). After the investigation was concluded, I was given the right to sue letter. I sued the company for discrimination in October 17, 1997 in the United State District Court, Western District of Washington, case number C97 –1656 WD.

A few months later, we reached an out of court settlement. The company paid me some money for mental anguish and emotional distress. After my lawsuit with the Freight Company, I vowed that I would never let anyone put me down again, or obstruct my progress in life. I knew that if given the right opportunity, that the sky was the limit to what I could achieve in life. But I have not been given that opportunity. It was so frustrating to be talented, but no avenue to express it, just because of discrimination.

MY JOB AT GOVERNMENT AGENCY OF WASHINGTON STATE

Before my experiences with discrimination, I have heard of discrimination and how some people were discriminated against. Then I wondered, if it was true that discrimination does exist, and does happen. But after the total number of discriminations I have experienced myself, it was a total shock to me that discrimination does exist, and some people even take the delight in practicing it and keeping it alive. You might not know the effect of discrimination in some one's life until you experience it yourself. However, I will never wish it on anybody. Discrimination was stressful, emotionally draining, demoralizing, and someone could be so depressed for a long period, if the person did not take adequate care of him or herself to remedy the situation.

After I had worked with three private companies and was discriminated against, I thought that the safest place to work to avoid discrimination was with government agency, since the government enacted and upheld the laws. I started working at the Government agency on March 24, 1999 as an Office Assistant in Department of Assessment. After one year, I applied and got another job as Fiscal Specialist 2 with the same department. When there was an opening for an Assistant Accountant job in the Central Payroll department, I applied for the job.

In May 2003, I was hired as an Assistant Accountant in the Payroll department of the Government agency. I was so happy that I could not find a word to express my happiness. I thought to myself, that I finally had a job where I would be able to apply the knowledge of what I acquired at the university to do my job. I loved my job so much that I look forward to going to work every day, and in catching the bus to work after I parked my car in the park and ride area. After I was hired as an Assistant Accountant, I settled down and tried to build my career around that job. However, Cindy, a black female Accountant, who had worked in the department for many years before I got there, was determined that my ambition would never materialize.

Cindy was my lead when I worked in that department, and she made my life a living hell ever since I worked there. She discriminated against me based on my disability, accent and national origin. She also abused and harassed me. She took some retaliatory actions against me, when I reported her to the management, and she made up false accusations against me. The management knew about those complaints, but instead of intervening to resolve the issues, they terminated me based on false accusations of what I did not do.

Cindy motives and hostile attitude towards me

When I was hired as an Assistant Accountant, the supervisor told Cindy, who was an Accountant to train me on how to use certain procedures in the department. Cindy told me that she would come and sit with me in my cubicle and spent some time with me, so that we would go over some topics in the computer together.

The first day she came over to my cubicle, she was so friendly and wanted to teach me many things. She told me to take some notes while she went through the procedures in my computer. Just before the first working week with her was over, she noticed that the kind of music I was listening to on my radio was not Rhythm and Blues (R & B) songs or rap songs. It was country music. By the way, Cindy was a black woman. She asked me what kinds of music do I like. I told her that I tend to listen to all kinds of music, like soft rock, Rhythm and Blues (R & B) music, Jazz, Reggae, country music and some classical music. I told her that I do not listen to hard rock music and some rap music, because they tend to give me a headache, and that my favorites are some soft rock and country music, because they tend to tell stories, and sometimes they tell some sad stories that would make someone to contemplate and shed some tears.

I thought the conversation would end there, but it did not. She asked me if I was married. I told her no. she asked me if I have some kids. I told her no. she asked me what kind of education I had before coming to work at the Government agency. I told her that I had a degree in Mathematics. She asked me if I was dating some one. I told her yes. She asked me if I was dating a sister (meaning if I was dating a black woman). I told her no, that I was dating a white woman.

While she was asking me all those questions, she was also busy with what she was showing me on the computer. But Immediately I told her that I was dating a white woman, her demeanor changed. From that moment, she made my life a living hell. That was the one question and one simple answer that changed my life for the worse, contributed to my downfall in the department, partially ruined my life, and made all the discriminations I had before very modest in comparison.

Just because I told her that I was dating a white woman, she abruptly stopped what she was doing, turned around and faced me. She asked me to explain to her, why most successful black men date white women. I told her that I did not know. She asked me if black women were not good enough for me to date, and does that mean that I did not like black women. I told her that I like all women, regardless of their races. She said, if that was the case, why was it that my girlfriend was white? I told her that both of us had certain things in common, and that we loved each other. She said that she understood the reason why I stated that I listen to soft rock and country music, and that it was because of the white woman I was dating. I told her that it was not for that reason, and that I did not like to listen to music that gave me a headache like hard rock and some rap music.

She used to stay two to three hours each day in my cubicle working with me until we went for lunch break, then after the break, she went back to her cubicle. However, after my answer about the woman I was dating, she told me that she wanted to take a fifteen minute break. After the break was over, I could see that her attitude towards me changed drastically. She used to log on to my computer and showed me the procedures while I took notes of what she was doing, but now she told me to log on while she guided me through what I was doing on the computer, and because of that, I was not able to take the notes of what she taught me. She did not care about the notes I took anymore, because she was mad at me.

That incident happened on Friday of the first week I worked with her. Then on Monday, which was one week after I started training with her, she told me that she would no longer spend some time with me, and that if I had any questions to ask her, that I would come to her cubicle for the answer. Remember my nightmare with this black woman started once I told her that I was dating a white woman. She told me that if a black woman was not good enough for me to date, why would she, who was a black woman, train me.

Sometimes when I asked Cindy some questions, she threw the questions back at me, thereby making me think and come up with the solutions. Sure, that was a way of learning, and once I came up with the solutions by myself, I did not forget how to solve the problem. However, in some questions where there were no clues, throwing the questions back at me was difficult to solve. I would like some clues on how to solve those problems, because without a clue on how to solve the problems, it then meant that I was back to square one when I asked the questions in the first place.

Cindy discriminated against me when she told me that my accent was terrible and heavy, and that she did not understand my English accent. She asked me where I learned my English before coming to the

United States of America. I told her that I learnt my English in Nigeria. She told me that I had to go back and polish my English again. She made those remarks known to my supervisor through some of the emails she sent to her and complained about my grammar, because my supervisor showed me the emails.

She used some foul and derogatory languages when she talked to me. At first, I thought that I would tolerate her verbal abuse and harassment, so that I could learn much from her, since she was the one assigned to train me in my job responsibilities. There was an incident when I asked her some questions, she said bullshit, you Nigeria motherfucker could not reason or think before asking me questions. She told me to go and figure it out for myself, and see if I could come up with the answer to the questions. She has used the word bullshit and motherfucker many times when she talked to me.

When she called me, Nigeria motherfucker, I was offended, because she used those words when I asked her a question. I did not make a big deal about it and was not angry, because I wanted to learn as much as possible from her regarding my job responsibilities. Some of my coworkers heard her use those words bullshit and motherfucker loudly in the office and reported the incidents to the supervisor, but she kept using those words sometimes when she talked to me.

Cindy discriminated against me because of my disability, when she instructed me to box W-2 tax form files. The first time she told me to box those W-2 tax form files, she knew I was disabled and could not do the job, but she insisted that I box those W-2 tax forms. I told her that I could not do the job, because of my disability. She told me that they had given me some slack for a long time, and that I should do it just like other employees or quit. Though I found it difficult when I boxed those W-2 forms, but to make sure I kept my job, I boxed all the W-2 tax form files in my cubicle and then moved them to the storage area. The second time she told me to box those W-2 tax form files, was before she went on vacation. She sent an email to our supervisor and to my coworkers, and listed the assignments she wanted each of us to do while she was gone.

The subject of the email was Coverage while out. It was sent to me and two of my coworkers, and copied to our supervisor. The three of us are Assistant Accountants with MSA payroll system. Part of the email that dealt with me stated, I quote " BK, Please find the time to get your desk organized, it's seems to take you a long time to find things when ask, because you have everything basically pilled together, also if there is extra time, you could go back to boxing the W-2's in the storeroom."

However, I had already told her that I could not do the boxing of those forms due to my disability. We had three Assistant Accountants in the MSA payroll system including myself. Then the question was, why did Cindy singled me out as the only person she wanted to go and box the W-2 tax forms in the storeroom? The answer was simple, it was because of her hatred towards me.

She stated that I should find time to organize my desk, because it took me a long time to find things when asked. That was false, because I was one of the most organized employees in the department. In fact, if I was not organized, I found it difficult to work fast and be accurate. My evaluation reports from different departments where I worked could vindicate the fact that I was well organized at my jobs. That email was written on January 23, 2004, and nine days after she came back from vacation on February 2, 2004, I was terminated from my job on February 11, 2004.

Cindy created some errors that did not exist and I was blamed for it

Cindy told me that she would make sure that I did not pass my probationary period. She used preparation of manual checks to accomplish some of that goal, because she created errors that did not exist in many of the forms that I prepared and gave her for approval, just to make sure that I accumulated many errors in my personal file and made me look incompetent.

Manual checks were given to the Government agency employees who did not receive paychecks on paydays, because they did not turn in their time sheets on time before the deadline, or maybe they were short paid on their paychecks. We used the Y adjustment forms to calculate the amount of the manual checks before we print them for payment to the employees.

Whenever I prepared the Y adjustment forms for the checks, one of my coworkers verified and approved them with their signatures signed at the bottom of the forms, which indicated that the calculation was correct. I gave the forms to Cindy for final approval. She circled all the errors she said that I made on the forms, and then gave the forms to my supervisor to document that I made those errors. My supervisor was not an Accountant, and she did not know much about the payroll codes on the forms. She took the photocopies of the forms with the errors, recorded the errors on my personal file that I made those errors, and then gave the forms back to Cindy. Cindy erased the circled errors she marked on the forms, signed her signatures for approval, and then gave the forms back to me to write and print the checks.

When I noticed how she created those errors and accused me of making them, I photocopied the documents I prepared before I gave them to Cindy, without her knowledge that I had those copies. One day our supervisor called me into the conference room and showed me the documents of those circled errors Cindy said that I did. When I showed the supervisor the photocopies of the forms that I prepared before I gave them to Cindy for approval, she realized that Cindy lied to her, because she purposely created those errors that did not exist, just to make me look bad and incompetent. From that day forward, my supervisor did not truth Cindy and had no confidence in whatever she told her about me.

The emotional anguish, pain and suffering that Cindy subjected me when I worked with her

Cindy was one of the worst bullies I had ever met in my life, because she intimidated and hurt me emotionally, coupled with the foul and profanity languages she used. When I worked with her, she subjected me to some of the worst humiliations, emotional and mental anguishes someone could ever endure.

- She was verbally abusive to me, teased and threatened me of losing my job, which brought down my morale and affected my productivity.
- She sabotaged my work, created errors that did not exist, and made me look incompetent.
- She humiliated and reprimanded me in front of other coworkers, whenever she felt I made a mistake and wanted to correct me.
- She sometimes set me up for failure with some unrealistic expectations, and then turned around and blamed me for the mistakes.
- She insulted me on many occasions and used profanity words when she talked to me.

- She caused my stress level to increase to the point that sometimes I questioned my self worth.
- When Cindy bullied and intimidated me, I was depressed, lonely and sometimes angry that my complaint about her to the management was ignored.

Some of Cindy Bully attitude towards me

- As I prepared to go to work in one winter day of 2003, the weather forecast for that day was that it would snow. So when I left home and drove to work, it was not snowing, but two miles closer to my work, it started snowing. Since I do not like to drive on snow, I called my supervisor and Cindy, and told them that I would be late for work. When I got to work, I parked my car on a passenger load and unload meter, went into the office and let them know that I had arrived for work.

  When Cindy saw me, she asked me where I parked my car. I told her that I used my handicap decal permit, and parked my car on a passenger load only zone meter on the street. I told her that I parked there, so that I could come in, worked for a while, then go out later, and move my car to another meter space when available.

  Cindy insisted that I go out and move my car, and then come in after I was done. That was not her business if I got a ticket or not. However, just because she was a bully and wanted to always be in control of what I did at work, she insisted that I do what she said. I went outside in the cold, and waited for about fifty minutes on the street in my car until I had a vacant parking meter, and then moved my car. She did not care that I wasted fifty minutes in my car doing nothing. All she wanted was for me to stay in cold weather.

- Another incident happened when I came to work one day, and I was at my desk working. Cindy came and told me that she was allergic, and had a cold because of the perfume that I was wearing. She told me to stop wearing the perfume. I stopped wearing it, just to make sure she would not blame me next time when she had a cold.
- One other incident happened when Cindy saw me using the telephone by the entrance door to our office. She told me never to use that phone to make calls any more. However, that was the same telephone used by my coworkers when they wanted to make calls, and Cindy never told them not to use that phone.
- Sometimes when I took my fifteen minute breaks or during my lunch breaks, I went into the conference room if it was vacant, to rest or read some books. If people schedule to use the conference room, and they found someone in there at their scheduled time, they could always tell the occupant to leave, since the room was about to be used for a meeting.

It happened that one day I was in the conference room during one of my break periods. Cindy came to me and told me not to use the conference room any more during my breaks or lunchtime. She told me to always go to the secretary and take permission before using the conference room. I told our supervisor what Cindy told me. The supervisor told me that she does not have any problem with me using the conference room whenever it was vacant. Anyway, I stopped using the conference room during my breaks just to avoid any confrontation with Cindy.

The day I was terminated from my job at the Government agency caught me by surprise. I knew that Cindy wanted me to be terminated, but I did not know that it would come that fast. The last day of my employment with the Government agency Central Payroll Operations was in February 11, 2004. When I came to work that day, I did not know that I was going to be terminated.

A few hours after I came to work, my supervisor called me into the conference room for evaluation of my work. When I had my previous evaluation reports, I was in the conference room with only my supervisor. However, that day, February 11, 2004, the Production Manager was with me and my supervisor in the conference room. After the Production Manager read my evaluation reports, and told me that I was terminated effective that very moment, my supervisor sheds some tears. She told the production manager that she wanted to extend my probationary period for few more months, and that she did not want to terminate me. The Production manager refused her request and terminated me. During my lawsuit with the Government agency, my supervisor was one of my witnesses that testified on my behalf for all the bullying abuse and humiliations committed towards me by Cindy.

After I was terminated, I put together all the relevant documents that were related to my claim for discrimination against Cindy and the Government agency, and then filed a complaint with the Equal Employment and Opportunity Commission (EEOC). The documents that I submitted to Equal Employment and Opportunity Commission proved what kind of discrimination, harassment and retaliatory actions Cindy committed towards me.

The hardship I went through during the period I was terminated was unbearable. After I was terminated from my job on February 11, 2004, I encountered numerous hardships. I almost lost my house, because I could not pay my mortgage. I did not have enough money to feed myself and pay for my bills. Therefore, I borrowed money from friends and family members and paid some of my bills. However, because of the late payments, my credit records were ruined. For those reasons, I could not get a new loan from the banks, couple with the fact that I did not have decent paying jobs for those years, because I had one temporary job after another trying to make both ends meet.

The ruling of the Equal Employment and Opportunity Commission (EEOC)

After I filed my case with the Equal Employment and Opportunity Commission (EEOC), it was thoroughly investigated, and in November 3, 2004, they concluded their investigation and determined that I was discriminated against. They recommended some proposals to the Government agency on how to settle the case. While I waited for the Government agency to make a decision on what to do about the Equal Employment and Opportunity Commission (EEOC) proposals to settle my case, I thought to myself, how could someone make any headway in life with the kind of work history that I had, and with the kind of setbacks I experienced? Therefore, I wrote the letter below to the Government agency management in February 14, 2005. I did not get any response from him, and that was when I decided to sue the Government agency in court. **Case number 06-2-25432-5 SEA, at King County Superior Court.**

My Address
Phone: (425) 37X-XXXX
February 14, 2005
The Government agency
Address

Dear Sir

The main reason I am writing this letter to you was to ask these questions, why me? Was I born to be discriminated against? Could someone tell me, when would the discrimination end? I am a disabled person who happened to be black, but discrimination has ruined my progress in life. From my personal experience, being black alone was a hindrance in some of the things I tried to do in life, then being black and a disabled person was an overwhelming impediment. I came to this country in 1980 from Nigeria to pursue my education in computer science, so that I would be useful to myself and contribute my talent to the society.

Due to unforeseen circumstances, both financially and physically, I graduated with a Bachelor of Arts degree in mathematics at the University of Washington in 1988. While going to school, I worked to support myself. In November 1992, I became a United States of America citizen. I had worked with three private companies and one government agency, all of them discriminated against me. These companies are as follows, (1) Industrial Laundry Company (2) Bank (3) Freight Company (4) Government Agency, in which you are the Executive.

I went to work for these companies in an entry level position, with the hope to build a career and grew within the companies, if given the opportunities. Boy was I wrong. In some of these companies, I applied for many internal job openings, but the jobs were given to some other people with less education and experience than I do, due to my race, national origin, accent, disability or with any other reasons, they found not to give me the jobs. While I was still working for some of those companies, I reported the discrimination practices to the Equal Employment Opportunity Commission (EEOC) or to the Washington State Human Right office, and had some documentation to prove it. These agencies intervened and wanted to resolve the issues between the companies and me.

As time passed by, these companies did not make any progress to resolve the issues, so the EEOC office gave me the right to sue letters. I never intend to sue the companies I worked for, but if my rights were violated with impunity, I had no other choice, than to go to court and ask for justice. Therefore, with the right to sue letters, I took the companies to court. Then later on, the companies settled the cases out of court. These are the companies with the court case numbers:

1. Industrial Laundry Company, Court case number 84-2-18060-9
2. Bank, Court case number 92-2-05177-0
3. Freight Company, Court case number C97- 1656WD
4. Government agency, Court case number 06-2-25432-5 SEA

Any time I went through any of these stressful encounters, I kept asking myself, what have I done in life to deserve these kinds of rejections and discriminations? They affected me socially, psychologically and emotionally. All I asked for in life was for someone to accept me for my personality and talent, but not the way I look or my race, so that I could at least try to live a normal life.

Going through those catastrophic incidents, was so demoralizing, that sometimes I wanted to stop striving in life. Then again, I asked myself, who would support me if I did not work to support myself? I did not want to depend on welfare help to support myself. That was the thought that comes to my mind any time I tried to give up striving. Therefore, with some reluctance, I found the courage, picked up the pieces and moved on with my life, hoping that one day, things would get better and I would make headway in my life.

However, it appears as if anytime I tried to put the past behind me, and make a fresh start in my life, here comes discrimination showing its ugly head again. So having worked with three private companies and was discriminated against, I thought that the best place for me to work and be safe, was to work with government agencies, like the city, county, state or federal government. My intention was that since these are all government agencies and the government enacts the laws that governed discrimination, that I would be safe working in that environment, and would not be discriminated against. Then when the opportunity arises, I would be given the chance to build a career and grew within the agencies.

Though I have a degree in mathematics, but since I was very eager to work with any government agencies, so that I could avoid discrimination in my life, I applied for an entry level position with the Government agency in Seattle. I was hired as an Office Assistant 3 in March 1999. All I wanted to do was to get my foot in the door, as the saying goes, so that I could work my way up the career ladder if given the opportunity, and then retire my civil service career with the Government agency.

After about one and half years as an Office Assistant 3 in the department of Assessment, I applied for the position of Fiscal Specialist 2 within the same department. I was hired for that position in 2001. Since most of my duties were payroll functions, I was happy that I used part of what I studied in school to do my job, and it was more challenging than the Office Assistant 3 job.

The best way to describe how good I was at my job as a Fiscal Specialist 2 ,was for someone to review my personal evaluation reports from the three different supervisors that I worked with, during my stay in that department, and see what they said about me. Among other things, these evaluation reports would show that I got along with my coworkers very well, regardless of their race, national origin or religion.

In March of 2003, I applied for the position of Assistant Accountant in the Central Payroll department of the Government agency, and after some interviews, I was offered the job in May 13, 2003. I finally said to myself, that this was a dream come through. That I could use most of the knowledge I acquired in college in doing my job. When I woke up in the morning, I always looked forward to going to work and contributed my talent to whatever the day had to offer. I loved my job so much that sometimes I did some of my coworkers' duties, just for them to go on vacations or go on sick leaves. I never missed work, and for any of the days I took sick leaves, maybe I was seriously sick, went for surgery or it snowed. From the day I was hired in March 1999 until the day I was terminated in February 11, 2004, I took minimum vacation days. That was because I loved my job, and I loved going to work every day.

After I had worked with the Government agency for almost five years, I said to myself, that I had found a stable place to *work, where I would not be discriminated against. Boy was I wrong. It happened that the worst discrimination I had in my life was from a black woman, an African American woman. I never in my wildest dream thought that black people would discriminate against other black people, because all the other discrimination experiences I had was on my race for being black, National origin or my disability.*

This African American woman was an Accountant in the MSA section of the payroll system, and when I was hired as an Assistant Accountant, she was my lead and was assigned to train me in some aspects of my job. However, when I asked her certain questions relevant to what I did, she did not answer my questions or gave me any clue as to what to do to get the answers to those questions. I wrote to my supervisor and complained about the situation. When the problems were not resolved, I was later assigned to another coworker to help me out with the training. Still, this black woman kept interfering with my training. Sometimes she sabotaged my work just to make me look bad and incompetent. She knew I was a disabled person, but insisted that I boxed W-2 tax forms files, even though I told her that I could not do it.

Most of those atrocities she committed towards me was documented and given to my supervisor to intervene and resolve my problems. The management did not resolve my problems, but instead, I was terminated from the job that I loved, in February 11, 2004. This black woman bullied, and deed many depressing things to me. My supervisor wanted to extend my probationary period for few more months, but the Production manager refused. I asked her if I could be transferred to another section of the department, she said no. I had about three more days to complete my five years working with the

Government agency before I was terminated.

That February 2004, I went to the Equal Employment Opportunity Commission (EEOC) office, filed a discrimination complaint against the black woman, and gave them all the relevant documents that substantiated my allegation of discrimination. In November 3, 2004, after thorough investigations, the EEOC office made the determination that I was discriminated against. Part of the determination stated as follows quote " I have considered all the evidence disclosed during the investigation and have determined that there is reasonable cause to believe that the Charging Party was criticized and taunted during his training based on his national origin and disability, and that he was retaliated against for reporting the hostile work environment to management."

During all those periods, I did not hire a lawyer to represent me, because all I wanted was to resolve the issues, so that I would go back to my job and contribute my talent. I had worked for four companies, and all of them discriminated against me. I thought that I would be safe and protected from discrimination when I worked with government agencies, but that was where I experienced the worst discrimination in my life. So where else do I have to work to be immune from discrimination?

In the past, after I settled my discrimination lawsuits, I would just move on with my life and did not want to work for that institution any more. Then I would hope that the next company where I work, would not be like the previous one and discriminate against me, so that I would start my life all over again.

However, do I have to keep starting my life all over again any time I go through this kind of discrimination? I am getting older every day, and I need to plan for my retirement. If I kept walking away any time I sued a company for discrimination, when is the circle going to end. So as a matter of principle, and also based on the fact that I am getting older every day, and need to start planning for my retirement, I would not walk away this time from my job. If going to court was what it takes to get my job back, I would do so.

Someone looking at my work history, and the previous lawsuits I had with the companies where I worked in the past, might think that I love going to court. The answer is definitely no. Take for example, my case with the Government agency Payroll Department, I first went to the Equal Employment Opportunity Commission (EEOC) office and filed a discrimination complaint after I was wrongfully terminated.

During that period, I did not have a lawyer. Then when EEOC office made a determination that I was discriminated against, I still did not have a lawyer, and was willing to resolve my case with the Government agency without going to court. Throughout the whole investigation, the Government agency had some attorneys dealing with the case. It was only when the EEOC office, informed me that the reconciliation proposal had failed, that was when I hired an attorney to represent me. Like I stated earlier, I do not like to sue any company where I worked in court, but when my rights were violated with disregard to the laws, and the only option I had, was to go to court to seek justice, then I would do it. Because, I did not do anything wrong to that black woman to deserve how she bullied and harassed me on my job.

I am writing this letter to let you know how I was treated when I worked at the Government agency, and also asked this question again, why me? What have I done in this world to deserve *those kinds of discriminations? That I was born with black skin, was that my fault? That I had polio when I was a child, was not my fault either.*

Finally, all I asked my fellow human beings was to stop all the discriminatory behaviors they have towards me, so that I would try to live the little bit of life I had left in this world, and be useful to the society. I am very sorry to bother you with my problems. Thanks.

Yours Sincerely

Chibike Nwabude

The settlement of my case with the Government Agency

It was ironic that one of the federal government agencies, the Equal Employment Opportunity Commission (EEOC) investigated and determined that one of the state government agencies violated the law of discrimination against me. After the investigation of my case, the Equal Employment Opportunity Commission (EEOC) ruled on November 3, 2004, that the Government agency discriminated against me. They wanted to settle the case between the Government agency and me, so they recommended some proposals to the Government agency on how to settle the case.

The Government agency requested some time to go through the proposals and conduct their own internal investigation. When the reconciliation proposal was unsuccessful between the Equal Employment Opportunity Commission (EEOC) and the Government agency, the EEOC gave me the right to sue letter. It stated as follows, quote "You are further notified that you have the right to institute a civil action under Title VII of the Civil Right Act of 1964, as amended, 42 U.S.C. 2000e, et seq., and Title I of the Americans with Disabilities Act of 1990 against the Government agency."

I hired an attorney and filed a lawsuit against the Government agency in June 2006, and the court hearing date was set for January 28. 2008. A few days after the Government agency took my deposition in October 2007, they called my attorney and stated that they wanted to settle the case out of court. The mediation meeting between my attorney, the Government agency and me was held in October 19, 2007.

On the day of the hearing, both parties arrived at the mediator's office. The mediator sat both parties in different rooms of their office. Then she went back and forth between the rooms where I stayed with my attorney, and the room where the Government agency attorneys stayed, and relayed to the other party what was proposed and counter proposed to settle the case.

When the mediator walked into our room, my attorney gave her some supporting documents with the background facts about my case, and she in turn gave us some documents from the Government agency attorneys with some information about me to support their arguments.

One paragraph in the four page documents caught my interest when I read it. The paragraph stated as follows, that Nwabude is described to us by his former co-workers and supervisor as a pleasant, nice man. But during discovery, the Government agency learned that Nwabude has sued two of his prior employers and he has received settlement in both cases. Nwabude has also been involved in other litigation not related to his employment. Nwabude has alleged race and national origins discrimination claims in these other lawsuits in addition to failure to hire/promote. While at first blush a jury may be sympathetic to Nwabude, if a jury learns that he is a seasoned litigant, he will quickly lose this advantage.

After I read that paragraph, I showed it to my attorney. Now let us analysis that paragraph a little bit. I was glad my co-workers and supervisors described me as a nice and pleasant man. It stated in the paragraph that I sued two of my former employers. The number was wrong, because it was three former employers, and if the Government agency were included, that would be four employers that I sued for discrimination. I do not care if the jury learned that I was a seasoned litigant or not, because one fact should be clear about me in those lawsuits. If someone does any wrong to me, and I perceived that as injustice, or if someone discriminate against me, I would fight for my rights, and against any injustice. You should be rest assured, that I would take any legal action against that individual, or company and seek for justice.

The mediator asked my attorney and me what our demands to settle the case were. We told her the monetary amount we wanted for pain and suffering, emotional distress and back wages. I also told the mediator that I would never settle my case, until I get my job back. The mediator then went and told the Government agency attorneys what we demanded for settlement. After a few minutes, she came back and told us that the Government agency did not want to rehire me to work with the agency anymore. She said that the Government agency had a checkbook with them, and that all they wanted me to do, was to tell them the amount of money I wanted to settle my case. She said that once I told them the amount, they would write me a check for that amount, and then settle my case that very day.

Once the mediator said that, I turned around and told my attorney that I would never settle my case for any amount of money without getting my job back. The mediator said that we are not sure that I would win my case in court, because we did not know how the jury would decide the case. She said that it was better for me to take some money and settle my case. My attorney requested some time to discuss with me the implications of what might happen if I did not take the money settlement, and the case goes to court. The mediator told us to signal to her when we were ready to continue the discussion, so that she would come back for our final decision.

I told my attorney again, that I did not care about the Government agency money, and that I would not settle my case until I get my job back. I told him that I rather go to court to get my job back, than to take the Government agency money and not get my job back. The reason was that, I did not do anything wrong to Cindy, the black woman who discriminated against me, and for that reason, I wanted my job back.

When I sued my former employers for discrimination, and we settled out of court, I did not work in those companies anymore, though I was offered another job to work with the companies. I always moved on and started a new life, and hoped that things would get better, but it did not. The next company I chose to work for, treated me even worse. Then, if I kept moving on with my life when those kinds of injustices happened, when would it end? When I am dead?

I told my attorney to remember, that the job discriminations I had before were with private companies. I decided to work with government agencies, with the hope that I would not be discriminated against, because it was the responsibility of the government to keep the laws. However, when the government discriminated against me, where then do I turn for justice?

We indicated to the mediator that we were ready with our decision. My attorney told her that I would not settle my case without getting my job back. The mediator repeated again, that I was not sure that I would win my case in the court if the juries decided it. I told her that

I was ready to take that chance, and if I lost my case in the court, it would be noted that I tried. However, I would not settle my case without getting my job back.

When she realized that I would not compromise on that very issue, she presented our demands to the Government agency delegations. When she came back, she told us that the Government agency stated that if they gave me my job back, that the amount of money they would give me to compensate for the pain and suffering, emotional anguish and back wages, would be drastically reduced. I told her that I do not care, as long as I get my job back. She went and told the Government agency delegations what I said. When she came back to our room, she told us that the Government agency delegations had decided to have some consultation with the other authorities at the Government agency, before they made the final discussion. Therefore, the meeting for that day was adjourned.

For the next few days, there were some telephone conference call negotiations between the whole parties. Finally, we agreed on the settlement amount, the kind of job I would be given with the step increases, from the year I was terminated to the date I started my new job at the Government agency. A few weeks later, I started my new job on June 12, 2008 with the Government agency.

My way of life

First, I have to say that I am very different from many people in different aspects of my life. I am a black disabled person. Meaning that, I could not run, jump, dance, walk fast or do many things that other people with good legs could do. Therefore, in that aspect alone, I am different. Mentally, I am different too, because the way I look at life is very different from the ways others do. I have an inventive mind, and like to invent or create things. I believed that I could have done more than some people if I was given the opportunity, but I wasted my talent due to injustices and discriminations.

I grew up and realized that I could not do many things in life, because I am a disabled person with limited use of my leg. I tried as much as possible to be the best in whatever I do or could do. I believe that people should work very hard for whatever goals and achievements they wanted in life. If someone wants to live a better life, they have to work hard to achieve that goal if there were no unforeseen obstacles along the way. Some of the obstacles I mean, are like discrimination, not given equal opportunity with others, and many other setbacks one cannot foresee in life.

I am a humble, honest, kind, caring and a loving person. I hate injustice in my life. I have no atom of jealousy in my bone. I rather suffer than see other people suffer. I have high respect for other people regardless of their age, race, national origin or religion. I strongly oppose anybody or group of people who impose their religious believe, ways of thinking, ways of doing things through manipulation or brainwashing, on other people. I am for justice and equality for all human beings. If I notice that someone or a group of people are practicing any of those things that I opposed, I become more skeptical in dealing with that person or that group of people.

I like to help people whenever I am in a position to do so, especially those in difficulties. I do not have much wealth in life, but with the little I have, I would contribute as much as I could just to help that individual or group of people. Sometimes it was stressful trying to solve other people's problems, but I do not mind, as long as I did my best to help whoever it was. Sometimes many people have taken advantage of my kindness and generosity, and treated me like a fool. But once I notice that kind of behavior, I would stop whatever I was doing for that individual or group of people without any explanation to them.

The way I treat other people, is the very way I expect them to treat me. Sometimes it does not necessarily happen that way, but that does not deprive me from doing good things to others. I could only do the best I could, and leave the rest to God.

I like to associate and have friends with people of all races. However, for someone to be my friend, it must take a great deal, because I do not have friends on face value, or just for the sake of it. Even when I do have friends, they are temporary friends, or what I called acquaintances. Meaning that, if those acquaintances did something wrong, regardless if the person is my friend or family members, I would tell them that what they did was wrong regardless of the consequences. Then, if that individual does not like it, or does not talk to me anymore, so be it. At least I told them the truth.

One of the main weaknesses I have in my life is that I am too caring and gentle. This is because I would be so absorbed in other people's suffering or pains, to the extent that I would sacrifice my own welfare in order to help and try to solve the problem of that individual or group of people. Even if they had done me some wrong, I still try to help them. Some people had taken advantage of my kindness, but I entrust that to God to judge.

In my prayers, I asked God to bless me with certain things in life, so that I could be able to help many people in need. I have vowed to God that if after giving me those things, and I do not use them to help people, please God punish me. However, it seems as if my prayers would not be answered, with the kind of setbacks and frustrations I had in all the efforts and progress I had made in my life. However, God's time is the best, and let your will be done.

My views on different topics of life

Discrimination

I have had my share of discriminations, that for the past thirty three years that I had worked for four different companies, both private and government agencies, I had sued all of those companies for discriminations. Those discrimination incidents were so stressful emotionally, very painful and demoralizing, because I felt as if I was been rejected by the society. Then when the government that is there to protect the whole of us against injustice, discriminated against me, where then do I turn for help? That was when I knew, I had to fight more for my rights and for the injustices perpetuated on me.

Do not get me wrong, I love this country in many ways, because of the many laws they have that protect the disabled people. This country is a land of opportunities, if someone is giving the opportunity to achieve it. Regardless if someone is a disabled person or not, if the right opportunities are given to that person, the sky is the limit to what that person can achieve. God, those opportunities have eluded me, and I am still struggling in life.

I am still grateful to this country, because I should have been dead a long time ago, if I was still living in Nigeria. The reason being that, disabled people do not have the kind of rights they have here in the United States of America.

Do you know there was a time in this society, if you are an educated black person without a job, and you are not decent looking, people are afraid of you, if they walk pass you on the street. Some people might even walk across the street just to avoid walking in opposite direction with you.

I do not like some of the systems in place here in the United States of America, whereby the hand that fed you, would turn around and destroy you. If you are a well educated black person, you become a threat, and might not be treated equally as other educated white people. Many of these stereotypes have changed a little bit, but there are still those perceptions out there. There are certain things that this society would do, to show you that even with your education and wealth, as long as you are a black person, you are still below certain ways of their life.

If only the white people know how much I love them, how I do not have any hatred against any one of them, or for anyone for that matter, then they should stop hindering my progress in life. Some of these discriminatory behaviors also applied to some black people, because some of them also have hatred against one another.

I love black people too, but if a black person discriminate against another black person, that is even worst, because it seems as if you are being betrayed by your own race. Also, I had experienced discriminations from both races, and found out that some black Americans thought that we blacks from African came to this country to take away from them the little opportunities that they have over here.

Discrimination is discrimination, regardless of what race or person that is perpetuating it.

Coming to the United States of America had always been my dream. Though not all the things that I envisaged to do and accomplish had turned out the way I wanted. However, what can I do? I always tried my best, and leave the rest to God. Only God knows what he has in mind for each one of us. I planned to use whatever achievement I had accomplished in life to help other people. But if it turned out, that what prevented me from achieving my goals in life was because I am a black disabled person, that hurts my feelings too much, that I will take the sadness to my grave, if that turned out to be the case.

There are discriminations in every society in the world in one way or another, and even in Nigeria. In Nigeria, if you are a Christian, you know that some Muslims would discriminate against you, because their religious belief is very different from your Christian way of doing certain things and vice versa. There are many different cultures in Nigeria, and what one culture practiced is very different from other cultures.

In Seattle, I call the kind of discrimination we have here, killing me softly kind of discrimination, and you might also call it silent discrimination. It is the kind of discrimination where some people would chat, smile and laugh with you as friends, coworkers or acquaintances, but behind your back, they are saying all kinds of nasty and derogatory things about you. Some of them would go to any length to jeopardize your progress in life.

I do not have any prejudice against anyone in my life. However, what I do have is skepticism, and being defensive against injustices. Whenever I experience prejudice or discrimination, I tend to withdraw a little bit from the source where that prejudice or discrimination came from, and then I tend to be on my guide.

I believe that, as long as there is life, I will keep striving and try as much as possible to do the best with the little that I have. I am a sensitive person, who is very sensitive to other people's feelings. If someone I love, or maybe someone that I know, or even a stranger around me is suffering, it hurts my feelings, and I feel their pain the most. In the process of thinking of how I could render help to them, and I do not have the financial means to help them out, that put lots of pressure and stress on me, to the extent that it affects me emotionally. I always ask God, to please help me to help others.

One could see that I tend to talk more about my experiences in the United States of America, because this is where I had spent most of my adult life. When I was in Nigeria, I did not have an intimate relationship with many women as I would have liked to, and I attributed that to my religious upbringing. The one time that I had sex with a girl, was just out of curiosity to see how it felt. It felt so good that I fell in love with her. However, as I was in the process to see if the relationship would blossom further, I left Nigeria when I got my visa to come and study in the United States of America.

Since I came to the United States of America, I had sex with a couple of women. I mentioned this fact, just to show that at the age of twenty four, when I was in Nigeria, I was not that sexually active, because I was brought up in a strict religious household. We are catholic, and my parents got the whole family so involved in the religion, to the extent that we prayed together every morning, or went to church before we do any daily activities, and also prayed together at night before we go to sleep. Due to that kind of upbringing, I did not have too many female friends. I missed that aspect of my life, because I would have liked to have many female friends.

One of my prayers to God, was that I would get the opportunity to use my talent to do many things in my life before I die. I also prayed and hoped that it would not be long, because I am getting older with every day and year that passed me by. I love my family members so much, that I would like to do some special things for them now that they are still alive, and especially to all the people that are in need of help.

Unfortunately, my father died, and I did not do many things for him, as I would have liked to do before his death. I am praying for God to bless me with some fortune, so that I could accomplish some goals, and help many people in the world before I die. But I do not know when, or if I will ever be fortunate enough to have the fortune, or wealth to help some people in need, and it might not even happen in my lifetime with the way things are going in my life. One obstacle after another.

Religion

My parents are religious people, and they instill in us the religious values of how to be humble and caring towards our fellow human beings. When we were kids and lived closer to the Catholic Church, my parents made sure that we went to mass every morning before we do our daily activities for that day. If we do not go to church due to unforeseen circumstances, we prayed together before doing our daily chaos. We also prayed together before we go to bed at night.

Before my father died at the age of ninety two, all his sensory organs were functioning great, and he rarely fell sick. In fact, we are all very grateful to God for his health, and for the kind of life he lived. Since he was so religious, our family benefitted a lot from his prayers.

My views on religion is that I believe in God, and knowing that we can die any time, I always try to prepare myself for that ultimate time of death, since we will be judged by our deeds on this earth. All over the world, there are many atrocities, discriminations, injustices, and all these are being committed in the name of God. That is the reason, I am so skeptical about some religions and the people that practice it. However, I still go to the church to pray and thank God, for all the graces and blessings I had been given so far on this earth.

Whenever I see people suffering, I like to put myself in their shoes or positions, and then I ask myself, supposing that was me, what would I do? Those kinds of thoughts always drive me to do everything legally possible to help that person or group of people, and I always try to remedy their situation. If it required me sacrificing what I have in order to help the person or group of people, I would do so.

What I hate the most in this world is injustice. I cannot stand seeing some people persecuted unjustly. If certain things were not done in a just manner, it hurts my feelings. It hurts me the most, because I knew that if I was given the opportunity, and I was fortunate to have the means or wealth to help others, I would give the last penny I have to relief the suffering of any person around me, and then suffer the consequence of being penny less. As long as I transfer their suffering to myself, instead of them suffering, that is okay with me.

In fact, after seeing some of the injustices and atrocities been committed in this world, I just asked God one question, why was I created in this world only to be witnessing all these inhuman things happen, and not able to help them out? I keep asking God, to use me in any way possible, so that I could help as many people as possible before I die.

I always pray to God, to please show me the vision of what he wanted me to do on this earth, so that I can be an example of how a person should treat his fellow human being. Whatever religion any person chose to practice is okay with me, and I respect that religion, as long as that religion does not advocate violence, beating women and the killing of other people with suicide bombs.

Politics

I like to read the news about politics sometimes, but I do not like to get personally involved in it. Though I tend to vote for certain candidates that I like their views and principles, but I do not like politicians, or the political party that thinks that we are stupid, and try to win elections through fear. That is, they would say that if you do not vote for their party, that bad things would happen, or that their party loves the United States of America more than others do, or that they defend the United States of America more than the other party does, or that they are more patriotic than others are. I do not like when certain politicians win their election in an unjust manner, or when the Justices had to step in and decide the election of the people.

Homosexuality

In the Good News Bible, Catholic study edition, it was written in Leviticus Chapter 18 verses 22, quote "No man should have sex with another man, and God hates that."

You shall not lie with a male as with a woman. It is an abomination. (New King James, Leviticus 18:22). Other Translations Leviticus 18:22.

You may not have sex relations with men, as you do with women: it is a disgusting thing. (Basic English Bible)

Homosexuality is clearly condemned in the Bible. However, some people have argued that the Bible specifically stated that man should not have sex with another man, and that it did not say that woman should not have sex with another woman, and as such, women are excluded from the quotation. We know that the Bible quotations referred to both genders, but that shows how different people interpreted the words in the bible.

Let us take a closer look to some of the sentences that the societies use as it relates to same sex. You might have heard some women say the following, I am going to see my girlfriend tonight, or I am going to one of my girlfriend's baby shower, or I am going out with my girlfriend to a movie, or I am going to have dinner with my girlfriend tonight.

People hearing those words, do not assume that the female saying them is a lesbian. We just know that the person saying those words would do what she said that she would do with her girlfriend. That does not mean that she is having sexual relationship with her female friends. Only a small percentage of females that say those words have sexual relationship with their partner, but the majority of the females that said those words are not in a relationship with their female friends.

Now let a man say any of those sentences with the word boyfriend in it, and notice the difference in meaning. For example, if a man says, I am going to my boyfriend's house, I am going to have dinner with my boyfriend, or I am going to a movie with my boyfriend. People hearing those words automatically think that the person saying those words is homosexual. If you are a man, you do use the word boy with friend together to refer to your male friends, because once those two words, boy and friend are used together, the meaning changes. That implies that the person might be homosexual. Therefore, to avoid what people might think, that the person saying those words is homosexual, men just say, I am going to see a friend, or I am going to have dinner with a friend etc.

You can see how societies view the use of those words, girlfriend of females, and boyfriend by males to mean different connotations. Therefore, using the word girlfriend by a female to another female is acceptable, and it does not imply that the person that said those words is a lesbian. However, the reverse is the case for a man.

I am a Christian, and I have some religious beliefs regarding homosexuality, but that does not mean that I should impose my beliefs on other people who do not believe in religion, or in God. For that reason, people should be able to do what is morally right for themselves, and should not be judged by our own standards. People should live their lives whichever way they want. They should also get all the civil rights benefits that every citizen have, because we are all created equal, and they should not be discriminated against in any way, shape or form. I do not know why people are homosexuals, and I am not here to judge any one's way of life. I am not God.

Capital punishment or death penalty

Nobody should kill another human being, no matter how grievous the offense committed might be. However, in self defense, when your life is in danger, you have the right to defend yourself, because someone else is about to kill you.

Any person who intentionally kill someone should be killed too, if it is proven beyond a reasonable doubt that the person committed the killing intentionally. I do not see any rationale in killing another human being.

Some people might argue insanity after they kill someone in order to get away with murder. If they are proven to be insane and then committed murder, they should be put in jail for the rest of their life. However, we should try to avoid people with mental issues from getting a gun in the first place.

Before someone is sentenced to death, we have to be sure that we are not putting an innocent person to death, for the crime they did not commit. It had been proven that some innocent people were put to death for the crimes they did not commit. Based on that fact, I think that people that committed murder should spend the rest of their life in jail.

Hitting your spouse/girlfriend or boyfriend

If people are boyfriend and girlfriend, or married couples, the man should never hit the woman and vice versa. I do not see the reasoning in beating up someone that you love, and after a while, you ask that same person, let us make love or have sex. It does not make any sense to me. People could argue as much as they want in any relationship, but it should never get to the point of hitting one another.

Injustice

I will like to live a healthy long life and then die a natural death that is of natural causes. However, with the way things are going in my life, I just have the feeling that I might not die a natural death. The reason is that, I am too outspoken, and I do not like injustices in any way, shape or form. I have been a victim of injustices and discriminations for the major part of my life. When someone stands out to oppose injustices, that person's life might be in jeopardy. The fear of being killed by someone should not prevent me from speaking the truth, fighting for justice and doing God's will. Therefore, if I die doing those things that is part of my life, that is okay with me and my God.

Smoking

I do not smoke cigarette or involve myself with whatever kind of smoking. Some Smokers are my friends, but I tend not to fall in love with females that smoke, because they have bad breath. Kissing them is just like kissing ash, and I do not want to get second hand smoking disease.

Drinking

I do not drink beer or alcohol, but I do drink wine cooler sometimes. I think that people should drink in moderation, and they should not drive while intoxicated. Anyone who drives a car while intoxicated, and then end up killing someone, should be put in jail for some number of years, because they knew that they should not drive under the influence of alcohol.

If someone is drunk, then drives, and gets into an accident, that is a premeditated and intentional behavior, because that individual knew what he or her deed. You could get drunk as much as you wanted in your home, but never in public places. If you drink in public places, make sure you have someone to take you home when you are drunk.

My social life

I like to socialize with people, especially with females. There is something special and magical about women and their pretty bodies, and I love pretty women. I like to make people laugh sometimes, and I am very considerate about other people's well-being and feelings. I am a quiet person, and I do like my space. I do not like to talk too much, and I do not like to argue just for the sake of argument. I am smart and intelligent, and do not like when someone messes around with my intelligent.

Sometimes people take my quietness to mean that I am dumb, and I tend to go along with their assumption, and even give the impression that I am stupid. However, when someone tries to take advantage of the so called dumbness, that is where they make mistakes, and they would see a different part of me that they had not witnessed before. That was the reason I said that I do not like people messing with my intelligent. I do not like to inconvenience people, and as such, I do not like when someone does the same to me. I am a very compassionate person, who is very caring, humble, generous, loving and honest, and could give up my welfare or my way of life, so easily for the welfare of other people.

I am a sensitive and an emotional person. Sometimes when I am at home, in my car, walking, sitting or doing some daily activities, I sometimes cry internally, and if nobody was around me, tears would pour out of my eyes. Even when I am in the church, there are certain songs I would hear from the church choirs, and tears would start running down my eyes. Some music does that to me too, especially some country music.

While I am crying and meditating, I sometimes ask God, why me? What have I done, or what did I do to deserve these hardships in life?

That was because my pains and suffering were getting worse every day. By that, I meant, that any time I was in the process of making any headway in life, something drastic would happen to me, and then set me back to where I started, and sometimes set me back worse than where I started.

In my prayers, I always ask God, if there was anything, I had done wrong, which I was not aware of, that he should let me know about it in any way possible, so that I could correct it. God, I recognize that one day I will die without accomplishing all the good things I set out to do in my life, because I was not blessed with fortunes, due to the obstacles I had in my life.

Then again, I would say to God, I am not bitter, is just that the suffering is too much, and I keep asking, when it is going to end. The pain and suffering I am referring to, are the difficulties of my life. I am not talking about my health, which was another issue of its own, because I am a disabled black person.

Sometimes, I lack confidence in many things that I do, and this was because of the many injustices I had in my life. Because of the many discriminations I had at my jobs and in my life, that made me thought sometimes that I was not good enough, smart enough or attractive enough to other people, and I would directly or indirectly be begging for the acceptance and for the love of people, especially if I care so much for them. **God, discrimination hurts, and it had devastating effects in my life.**

Occasionally I do not receive the loving and friendly feelings I radiant towards other people back. Some people had done too many wrongs to me, and because I did not retaliate or pay them back with the same wrong they did to me, some of those people turn around and call me a wimp. That is okay, because two wrongs do not make a right. I do not mind being called a wimp, as long as I am doing the right things in life and in the eyes of God.

My health

For the past thirty years, I had a chronic ulcer on my right leg, where I wear a brace due to the polio I had when I was a child. This ulcer had healed and opened up repeatedly, that it was too frustrating to live with. I have had one surgery after another surgery, for a total of five surgeries on this ulcer, only for it to heal, and after some months, it opened up again. If the five surgeries were added with the other major treatments that did not require surgeries, that would be more than ten treatments at different hospitals.

During some of those surgeries, my family members did not know that I had the surgeries. Sometimes, I told them after I had the surgeries and was resting at home. I knew that if I had told them in advance that I was scheduled to have some surgeries, that some of them would volunteer to come and stay with me during the surgeries.

On one or two occasions when I told my senior sister about the surgeries that I had, she advised me to tell her in advance any time I wanted to have a surgery, so that she could come and stay with me during the surgery. But I did not like to be a burden to anybody with my illness, or cause any emotional stress to anyone, and that was the reason I did not tell anyone sometimes, that I was about to have surgery.

In the hospitals, just before the surgeries, some of the doctors would ask me if I had a family member or a friend with me in the waiting room, so that they would update and give them progress reports about my surgery. I told them no. When I was rolled into my room after the surgeries, it felt so lonely, because I did not have anyone to comfort me. But I had strong faith in myself, and the only person I had with me was my God. All I could do was pray to God, and let his will be done.

For the fact that I have experienced many medical treatments on this leg ulcer for the past years, and it had not healed permanently, was so troublesome to me, that it hindered some of the things that I wanted to do in life.

I adapted myself to the discomfort and pains of the leg ulcer, and from my reactions and feelings, the people around me did not know what I was going through in life, unless I told them. If I had told my brothers and sisters about my leg ulcer, they would be sorry and sympathize for me. Though that was a good gesture on their part, but that would not solve my problems, and I did not want to turn over my stress to them. I had given my way of life to God, and I had prepared myself spiritually with my God, that whenever it is my time to leave this world, I will gladly do so with the help of God.

My senior sister was very sympathetic for me whenever I was sick. Sometimes she became so worried and stressed out about my illness, that she got ill herself. When that happens, I would be so stressed to the point that I blamed myself, that I was the one that caused her illness. I love my sister, and I did not like to see her sick. Therefore, to avoid that chain reaction, the best thing for me to do, was not to tell her about my illness.

My youngest sister lived with me for about six months in 2010. I did not tell her that I had an ulcer on my right leg, and that I received medical treatment throughout the period she lived with me. When she stayed with me, I scheduled my doctor's appointments after I got off work at 2:30pm. Once I got off work, I drove to my doctor's appointment, and they dressed the ulcer wound before I went home.

Sometimes when I got home late, my sister asked me the reason why I came home late. I told her that it was due to the traffic jam on the roads, or that I worked some overtime hours at my job. She is the kind of person, once you tell her about your illness or problems, she would worry and be so sympathetic for the person. I do not like to see her stressed out because of me.

I appreciated someone feeling sorry for me for my illness, but I am not going to dwell in sympathy, or pity to survive. I knew that if I did not take good care of my leg ulcer, that it might kill me, if it becomes incurable with certain kinds of bacteria. Therefore, that was the reason I followed every treatment recommended by my doctors.

In 2010, when my Father died, I regrettably did not attend his funeral services in Nigeria, because I was still receiving medical treatments for my leg ulcer. When I told my brothers and sisters that I was not going with them for the funeral services, they understood my predicament, and they thought that it was because of my disability, but they did not know about the treatments I was receiving for my leg ulcer.

From 2008 to 2012, I had some major medical treatments on my leg ulcer, and the last surgery I had on the ulcer was a laser surgery in May 2012. The ulcer healed after the surgery, but opened up again after a few months. When my younger sister came back to stay with me for a few months in 2012, I was still receiving medical treatment for the ulcer, but again, I did not tell her about it. When she was married and moved to stay with her husband in one of the cities on the east coast, she still did not know about my leg ulcer treatments.

On September 2012, I tripped and fell at work and injured my elbow and my hand. I received some medical treatments for those injuries. In November 2012, I had surgery on my hand due to the fall I had at work, and was still receiving therapy treatment for the hand when we celebrated New Year 2013. Therefore, I started the year 2013 with the medical treatments I received at two different hospitals. In one hospital, I received treatment for my hand, while at another hospital, I received medical treatment for my leg ulcer.

Sometimes when I had two doctor's appointments in one day, I went for my hand therapy treatment appointment in one hospital, and once I was done there, I drove to the other hospital for my leg ulcer treatment. By the time I was done with those treatments, all I wanted to do was just go home and rest.

After a few months, the medical treatments that I received from the hospital for my leg ulcer was so encouraging and assuring, that every day that passed, I discovered that the ulcer was healing. On February 8, 2013, when I came for my leg ulcer treatment, the Unna boot dressing on my leg ulcer was taken off, and the ulcer had healed completely.

The doctor came in and told me that he had discharged me that day, because my leg ulcer had healed. I was so happy and grateful to all the nurses and doctors that took good care of me at the hospital to make that happen. Then when I got into my car, I prayed and thanked God, that my leg ulcer had healed, and for the new lease on life, he had given me.

Therefore, I would say that February 8, 2013 was one of the happiest days of my life, because that was the day the nightmare of my leg ulcer ended. I vowed that if my leg ulcer ever heals, that I would make sure that I never suffer it again. I have kept that promise with the medical instructions I was given. The alcer had healed permanently.

My Father

My parents are humble, religious, compassionate, generous, caring, loving and kind people. They are the type of parents that anyone would ever wish to have, and I am very proud of them. My father has two brothers and one sister. When his two brothers died, he took it upon himself to support the children of his brothers. He also helped anybody that needed help, to the detriment of our family welfare.

Sometimes we blamed him for neglecting us just to take care of other people's problems, and he does not like injustices. I could say that it was from him that I picked up my habit of helping people regardless of my own welfare, and I do not like injustices in my life.

My father was a peacemaker, who does not like trouble. He was a man of wisdom, who liked to spread that wisdom to other people. I remembered one incident when he wrote some detailed articles, entitled Article of peace, to our relatives on how certain wrongs that happened in the past among our clan's men had to be corrected, so that everybody could live amicably and in harmony. Our relatives thanked him for his foresightedness. We had some meetings, and many disputed issues were settled.

Though my father never received a formal university education, but the type of education he had in those days to earn him a job, as a

Railroad engineer, could be comparable to the university education degree these days. His English and writings were much better than some of the English and writings of some people that went to formal universities. My father did not go to a formal university, but he made sure that his own children would receive the education we wanted, and as far as our brains could hold, the sky was the limit to our education. Sometimes my parents could not afford to pay our school fees, and he would borrow some money from friends, just to pay our tuition fees.

He believed that a mind was a terrible thing to waste, and that with education and knowledge, someone could always get a job and be able to afford what he or she wants in life, if given the opportunity. His advice to me, at my early age, was that education was my biggest asset, since I am a disabled person. He told me that I could live comfortably with a nice job, after I acquired my education. With that advice from my father, I tried to learn and do the best I could in whatever I did.

The name of my father was Nwabude Ositadima Nworjih. Nwabude was his first name and Nworjih was his last name. Nworjih was the name of his father, whom I did not get to know before he died. My father did so much for our family, and sometimes he sacrificed his own welfare just to make sure that we are comfortable and had most of the things we wanted. We loved his devotion to God, the caring and the dedication he had for helping people in need.

Because of all the good things that my father had done for us, and also due to the fact that I did not want all those things to be forgotten without him being recognized, I decided to honor him by taken his first name as my last name, so that he would not be forgotten in my life. That was the reason I changed my name to Chibike Ifechinelo Nwabude. By the way, my first name used to be Chukwubike.

However, I noticed that it was a long name to pronounce, and since Chukwu and Chi meant the same word God in Igbo language, I decided to shorten my first name to Chibike. So all I did was to replace the Chukwu with Chi, and you have Chibike.

In many conversations I had with my father, he told me that I was the person closer to his wisdom, personalities and philosophies of life. He told me that the touch had been passed on to me, and for me to embrace it, and make good use of it. That is what I had been trying to do with my life.

On New Year's Day of 2010, as every member of my family was celebrating that day, I was not happy, because of the kind of feelings I experienced. Those feelings were that something terrible was going to happen in our family. I had never experienced that kind of feelings in my life before. During the conversation I had with my senior sister, I told her about the kind of feelings I had for the year 2010, and that something terrible was going to happen in our family. She told me not to have those kinds of thoughts, and that nothing would happen. I told her, that I hope so.

The year 2010 was a terrible year for our family, because that was the year my father died. My mother's sister died in January 2010. She was the only sister my mother had left among all of her family of three sisters and two brothers. My mother's parents died long time ago and I was only able to know and met her father when I was a kid before he died.

The death of my father

My father was born in September 1918, and he was 92 years old when he died in February 23, 2010. Though I mourned the death of my father, because I loved him dearly, but at the same time, I was happy that he lived a good, happy and long life before he died. If many fathers were like my father, I think the world would be a better place to live and cherish with each other.

The tribute I wrote in honor of Father's death

Nwabude Ositadima Nworjih, my dad and my mentor, though you are gone, but your love, caring and sacrifice for all humanity will never leave us. You will never be forgotten.

Our father's greatest joy in life was helping those who were less fortunate in life. In fact, one of the ways to lighten up his face with a smile, was the mention of praise be to God. The religious and Christian way of life that you taught us have guided me through some rough times and tribulations. For that, I thank you Dad.

You did not mind that you did not get the best education, as long as your children and the people you tried to help in life, were afforded the opportunity to excel in whatever they do. It did not matter if your work was not what you had hoped for, as long as it gave your children the means to build their own futures. You willingly accepted all those working hours away from home, so that we would live comfortably.

We have a life that was paid for in advance, through the difficult and dedicated efforts of a loving and caring father, who traded the best years of his own life, just to make sure we would have the best years of ours.

Father, though you are gone, but your wisdom and humanitarian activities will never be forgotten. That was one of the reasons I changed my last name few years ago, from Nworjih to Nwabude to reflect your first name. So that I would carry, the legacy of what that name stood for, caring, loving, kindness, humbleness, justice for all etc. through the rest of my life.

As we say goodbye, I want our Father's life to be remembered as a man who cared deeply for the welfare of his fellow human beings. Dad, we love you, and you will be dearly missed. Thanks for all you have done for us. May your soul rest in peace.

Chibike Ifechinelo Nwabude

My MOTHER

My mother was the glue that bonded our family. She was a special woman in my life. I do not know where I would have been today without my mother, and the sacrifices she made for me. Anybody who has a disabled child knows how difficult it is to raise that child. My mother gave me all the special attention I needed in order to nourish me into manhood, and if there were anything I would do to repay her for all the things she did for me, I would do it.

I was a disabled child, and my mother never gave up on me. That I am walking today, was because of the sacrifices, caring and love that my mother gave me. During the Nigerian civil war, my mother knew that I could not run if the city where we lived went into panic mood, and people started running for their lives, because the city was about to be taken over by Nigerian troops. She arranged that I leave earlier with our uncles and nieces on her side of our family, and I had to reunite with my parents more than one year later, after we separated in different cities.

My mother could look at me and tell if something was bothering me or not. When we needed something from our father, and we perceived that we might not get it, we go through our mother to get those stuffs. My mother would go without her basic needs in life, just to make sure that we had what we wanted and be happy. She wakes up early in the morning, prepared breakfast for the family, and then prepared the foods she sold at her restaurant. She also cooked for the whole family at noon and at night, without any complaint.

I do not know where to start to list all the things my mother did for me in particular, and for my brothers and sisters in general. I love my mother so dearly, and would not substitute anybody or thing for her. That was the reason, when she was sick with knee injuries and needed knee joint replacements, I made sure that she received the best medical treatment United State of America could afford.

I never in my wildest dream thought that my mother who nurtured me since my childhood, when I had polio, would herself suffer leg injuries that required total knee replacement on both knees. After she had the surgeries, she was able to walk moderately with no pains at all.

During the time my mother had her surgeries, I went from having a job and working, to collecting unemployment benefits. After my unemployment benefit was exhausted, I applied and collected some social welfare benefits. Since I did not work during that period, I had all the time to take care of my mother after she got out from the hospital.

Words could not express the kind of suffering I went through during that period. However, I was glad I did all I could just to help my mother recover from her surgeries. I do not know any other person I would have sacrificed that much time and care, but for my mother. That was because she gave me an unconditional love and care when I was a child with polio and needed her the most.

A few years later, she suffered some major setbacks in her treatment, and one of her legs was amputated. However, I was working at the time her leg was amputated, but I stood by her all through her stay at the hospital, even though I had to go to work every morning.

My name is Chibike Ifechinelo Nwabude. I have already explained the reason why I changed my last name from Nworjih to Nwabude to reflect the first name of my father. I also changed my middle name from Victor to Ifechinelo, just to reflect my mother's first name, Chinelo. I knew that men do not go by the name Chinelo, so what I did was to add Ife to Chinelo to make it masculine. Therefore, Ifechinelo, means whatever God is thinking and has in stock for us will happen regardless of whom we are. By changing my middle name to Ifechinelo, meant that I would never forget my mother, just like my father. Because any time someone mentions my name, I thought of my parents.

In fact, I would have been sad and depressed if the polio I had would have happened to any member of my family. That was because I do not like to see any of them sad or depressed. It was okay that I was the one that went through those childhood pains. But to be honest with you, sometimes I wished that those pains were over, so that I could at least live a normal life.

When I was a child, I had all kinds of medical problems. I knew that I was different from other kids and would never enjoy much of the things that other healthy kids enjoyed. However, my mother helped me, and made sure that I enjoyed most of those things. Mother, all I could say was that I am very grateful for all the things you did for me, because without you, I would not have been able to walk today.

My siblings

I have five brothers and four sisters, but one of my beloved sisters Chinelo, whom I love and cherished so dearly, because she was very kind and caring, died as a result of food poisoning. In fact, I do not have any words that could describe how I loved her. All the characteristics that I have, being humble, gentle, kind, compassionate, does not like trouble, sensitive to peoples suffering and caring, she had them all and even more. She was even better than I was, and could do anything to help anyone in need. She would give up things that she liked and would use for herself, just to please other people.

I love all my family members, but this particular sister of mine Chinelo, was very dear to my heart, because we have many things in common. When she died, it seems as if part of me died even to this day. The day she died, I had just spent a nice warm afternoon with her that day, because she lived in bordering school and visited us from school.

I helped her carry all the stuffs she bought like beverages, books and other food items she would use in school, and then escorted her to where she caught the taxi back to school. When she entered the taxi, I said goodbye and safe journey to her, not knowing that it was the last time I would see and talk to her again in my life.

When she visited us that afternoon, my mother was not at home, because she traveled to Zaria, a city in the Northern States of Nigeria to check on our rented house. She was still there when my sister died, and was not told about her death, so that she could finish all the business transactions, she wanted to accomplish there. Three days after my sister's death, my mother came home. When she was told of her death, she was devastated, because my sister Chinelo, was so dear to my mother. My sister had all the qualities of my mother and both of them shared the same first name.

We were told that when my sister came back to school that afternoon, she fainted in the cafeteria after she ate the school dinner. She was admitted to the hospital, but was pronounce dead on arrival. When some of my sister's schoolmates came to our house and told me that my sister, whom I had spent that afternoon with, was at the hospital unconscious, I did not believe my ears.

When I went to the hospital and saw my sister, I was dismayed and surprised that her body was covered with white cloth from head to toe, to prevent someone from seeing her face. I went to the doctors and told them to do something to help my sister. But they sat me down and told me that there was nothing they would have done to help her, and that she was dead before they brought her to the hospital.

I believed that a schoolmate poisoned my sister, and that was the reason I am so skeptical about some people or some friends today, because some people use that method to retaliate against someone that did them wrong. Here in United States of America, if someone stops breathing, they do not say that the person is dead out right. At least they would try to revive the person through mouth-to-mouth resuscitation, or cardiopulmonary resuscitation (CPR). In those days in Nigeria, the opposite was the case. Once someone stops breathing, they would pronounce the person dead.

To this day, I still hold the memories of my sister's death very vivid in my mind, because she was so dear to me and I truly loved her. The day she was buried, her body was transported from Enugu where we lived to our village, where she lay in state and people paid their final tribute to her. The burial place was about three quarters of a mile from our house. Vehicles do not drive in that kind of roads, so some men carried her body to the burial place. The mourners told me not to go to the burial place because of the distance. I said to myself, no matter how rough the road was, and how far the distance was, that I would pay the last homage to my dear sister. So I walked to the burial place. By the time I got there, they had already placed her body six feet under the ground, and was about to cover it with sand when I arrived there. I was speechless. All I said and thought to myself, was that I would never see my dear sister any more.

I had begged God to take my life first, instead of the lives of my brothers and sisters or my parents. In fact, after the death of my dear sister, the way I view life now is very different. I could sacrifice my own welfare in other that my brothers and sisters could get what they wanted. As long as they are happy, I am happy, but if they are sad and I am happy, that is not okay with me.

My brothers and sisters have also helped me in times of difficulties. I remembered sometimes when I did not have any money, and I called on any of them for help, they tried as much as possible to help me. We helped each other as much as possible, and my greatest joy in life was to see all the members of my family happy, because we were brought up with religious morals, and we loved and cherished one another.

I would rather trade places with any member of my family when they are in trouble or unhappy. My life had been filled with one disappointment after another, that I rather be the one having those misfortunes, than to see any member of my family go through what I went through in life. Any time I tried to make a headway in life, something drastic or catastrophic would happen, only to set me two times or more backwards. I have had so many disappointments in my life to the point that my self confidence hit rock bottom on many occasions, and sometimes, I started to doubt my own ability and self confidence to do certain things, and have them accomplished.

My sisters and brothers are kind, humble and caring. My senior brother has the heart of gold. He had done many things to help our family in general and me in particular. He was the one that made it easy for me to come to the United States of America. He was able to facilitate the whole admission process by telling me what documents to submit, and then followed it up after I submitted the document to the schools.

When I arrived in Seattle and stay at their home, he and his wife gave me a nice accommodation, and they made me feel at home. They had two cars, which they were using at the time. One day my brother came to my room, and we were discussing different issues, he told me that one of the cars was mine once I learned how to drive a car. I asked him if he was kidding, he said that he was not kidding. He told me that, since I am a disabled person, that I would use the car to go to school and go to work if I get a job.

The moment that he said that the car was mine, if learned how to drive a car, I said to myself, that it was up to me to prove to him that I could drive a car. He gave me the keys to the car and told me that he would help me learn how to drive. I was so happy for that brotherly gesture. So I took it upon myself to learn how to drive before the school started in September of that year. The first day I drove the car, my brother was in the passenger's seat and instructed me on what to do and not to do about driving, and showed me how to operate the dashboard gadgets in the car.

We drove through the remote streets of the city, and he saw how fast I picked up the driving lessons. The following day we went and got my learners permit. I gave myself about two months to get my driver's license. My brother drove with me about four times when I learned how to drive a car, and when he was sure that I had learned the basics on how to drive, he stopped riding in the car with me while I learned how to drive. During my practice drives, I drove the car through some remote streets, going from one block to another without much traffic.

One day as I drove from one block to another, I did not know that I had already gone out of the city limit of Seattle, and I was in another city called Renton. Since I was not familiar with the area, and did not know where I was or how to get back home, I drove to a nearby public telephone booth and called my brother. I told him that I was lost, and did not know how to get back home. He asked me to describe the area where I was, so that he could come and give me a ride home. After I gave him the description of the area where I was, I waited for about fifteen minutes, and he showed up where I was. He told me to drive my car and follow him behind, and we got home safely.

After that incident, whenever I was going for a practice drive, I took a note pad and a pen with me, so that I could write down the name of the streets where I drove, and then on my way home, I could retrace the streets and then find my way home.

After I received my license, I was able to drive myself to school and to work. One day I got off school, and was going to work that started by 4pm. As I was driving on the freeway, I saw a man that waved that he needed a ride. So I stopped and asked him where he was going? He told me that he was going to Seattle, and since I was going towards downtown Seattle, I told him to get in. He opened the car door and got in.

During our conversation, he must have detected my accent, and he asked me where I came from. I told him that I was from Nigeria. He asked me where was Nigeria. I told him that Nigeria was in Africa. Anyway, when I got to the Ballard area in Seattle, where he previously told me that he was going, he asked me if I could drop him off a little bit further, about eight more blocks away. I said okay. Remember, I had already gone out of my way to take this man to Ballard, and now he wanted another eight blocks to ride. When I approached a stop sign, I stopped, and was about to turn into the main road, when a big six wheeler truck hit the driver's side of my car, and it was damaged beyond repair. Here is the picture of my damaged car.

I hit my head so hard on the crushed driver's side door during the collision, that I thought that my head had exploded. I was bleeding from my head, and the man I gave a ride, opened the passenger's door and walked away. The driver of the six wheeler truck that hit my car, came and helped me. He called an ambulance that came and took me to the hospital.

When I was in the emergency room of the hospital, I thought to myself, how callous was the man I gave a ride, that he left me bleeding and walked away. May be he had something to hide, or he did not want to be recognized, so he walked away.

I was not that mad that my car was damaged beyond repair, because who knew what the man would have done to me if God did not intervene with that accident. I was grateful that God saved my life. May be the man would have done some harm to me if I had taken him to the place he wanted me to drop him off. To prevent that from happening, God intervened with that accident and prevented me from taking him to his destination. Since the car was a total loss, my insurance paid me some money that I used to purchase another used car.

I stayed with my brother for more than a year before I finally moved out and lived on my own. He had helped me during different times of difficulties. When I bought my house, I did not have any money to buy the refrigerator, washer and dryer, and many other items in my house. He and his wife loaned me some money to buy those things. When I was terminated from my last job, he helped me financially. In another incident, when I asked him for money, I could tell that he did not have that much money to help me, but the only money he had was in his credit card. He withdrew the money and gave it to me. I do not know how to repay him for all its kindness, except to pray and ask God to repay him immensely.

My second brother helped me a lot and I appreciated his help. He is very caring and compassionate. I recalled when I was terminated from my job at the Government agency, he called me on the telephone, and wanted to make sure that I was not depressed by what happened to me. He asked me if there were anything, he would do to help me. I told him that the amount of money I had would only pay for one month mortgage on my house, and that I might be foreclosed on my home if I did not pay my mortgage. He gave me some nice advices, and loaned me some money that paid for my mortgage for four months. I would have been foreclosed on my house without that money that he gave me, and for that, I am very grateful for his help.

My third brother is very dear to me, and hold a special place in my heart, just because of the incident that happened when we were kids and lived with our parents in Nigeria. It happened that one day both of us were in front of the housing complex where we lived. As we were chatting, a man was riding a bike along the side of the street, and something fell off from his bike, so I told my brother to go and pick the stuff and give it to the man who was riding the bike.

He had just handed the stuff to the man, and turned to start walking back to where I was, when a motorcycle hit him. The motorcycle hit him so hard that all of his front teeth were knocked out of his mouth and were scattered on the road. He stood up and rushed towards me, and was shouting, "I am going to die? I am going to die?" I told him no, but he lost quit amount of blood. He was rushed to the hospital where they stopped the bleeding, and he was told that those teeth could only be replaced with artificial teeth.

Today his front teeth are all artificial teeth, and this was because he performed a good deed to someone we did not know. Therefore, I still have a guilty conscience for that incident, because if I did not instruct him to go and give that stuff that fell off the bike to the man, he would not have been in the accident, and he would have had his natural teeth today.

You could see the reason why I said that I have a special bond with him. Also, he wanted to be a priest just like me, but he decided to get out of the seminary school and went to university here in the United States of America. He is now married with four children. I owe him dearly, because of the sacrifice he made to help a total stranger, but ended up losing part of his body for that.

My childhood Admirations

When I was a child, I was brought up in a religious household, and I admired priesthood and their holy way of life. I always wanted to live a holy life, because I could not stand injustices. With my disability, I thought that it would be impossible for me to join the priesthood. Then I chose to go to the university, have a career and then live a decent life if given the opportunity. With all the misfortunes I had, and how things had gone in my life, made me wonder if I made the right decision not to join the priesthood.

The thought of me living a holy life kept flashing back in my mind to the point that I decided to write some prayers and thought questions to God.

- Was the main reason why I am not married today had anything to do with my admiration for priesthood when I was a kid, and actually wanted to be one of them?
- Had my childhood ambition of becoming a priest, prevented me from falling in love and having a serious relationship?
- Did all the misfortunes, happened in my life, just to remind me of my childhood ambition?
- God, were you trying to make me fulfill my childhood

ambition, by not showing me a special woman in my life to marry? God, if I am not too old for my childhood ambition, let your will be done.

- I am in my late fifties and still I am not married. Am I destined not to have a serious relationship with a woman, and get married, because of my childhood ambition of becoming a priest?

- Please God, if that is what has happened, I pray that you change your mind, and let me get married. I love women, yes I do. I have prayed to you God, to bless me one day, with a special woman who is compatible with me in certain ways of my life, and then we can have kids and spend the rest of our lives together. However, God's time is the best, and let your will be done.

- God, if you know how lonely it had been in my life without a woman to love and cherish, then you should let me fall in love, and get married. You are God, you know that the anguish was too much for me to bear, but if that was the way you wanted me to live my life without a woman, I am willing to abide by it.

- God with tears in my eyes, please reconsider, I truly love women, and hope that someday you will show me the woman to love. I am in my late fifties, but I had not given up the hope of having a woman in my life and having kids. God, everything is possible with you, so you do whatever you want with my life. Please give me the strength and fortitude to handle it. However, I am not a Priest, but I had tried to live my life like one.

- Sometimes when I see a beautiful woman, I wished I was with that woman, and I would say to myself, God, oh God, what are you doing to me? Please help me, and give me that kind of woman. Again, I would say to God, let your will be done, because God's time is the best. If I will get married and have kids, one day you, God, will make it happen.

- God, if your intention was that I would live on this earth without a wife, I am not going to oppose it. But please God, I hope that is not the case. How I wish God, that you will change your mind and let me fall in love with a beautiful woman. God, I wish I had a lovely sole mate.

My views about women

The female body is God work of art. When they open their petals and let you into their world, is just like being in an extreme happiness. I love women, and I like to give them the affection, love, passion and care that they deserved. I pray and hope that one day God will bless me with a lovely woman to marry and have kids.

God I love pretty women. In as much as I love women, I could easily turn away from any woman if I felt that she does not deserve my love, because I do not want any trouble in my life. With my disability, I feel that I have little life left to live on this earth, and adding more stress to it will be too dangerous for my health.

Women are one of the beautiful creatures God created on this earth. They deserve to be loved and respected. I like making love to a beautiful and intelligent woman. The love and respect I have for my mother transcends to my love for women. If a man have a good woman who is not devious or try to bring him down in life, that is a precious blessing the man should cherish in his life, so that he can give her all the love she deserve, and vice versa.

Wives

Life is so lonely without a companion. So many times, I have woken up in the middle of the night wishing that I had a female companion by my side. But that aspect of my life had been denied from me for a long time. One of the reasons why I had not been married, or rather why it has taken me this long to get married, was because of my financial situations.

I had already elaborated how my job history affected my financial instability, which in turn affected my lack of decision in getting married. Any time I planned to have a serious relationship or planned on getting married, I had one setback after another. Either I was laid off from my job, or I was terminated, because of the discriminations I had on my jobs. Sometimes, I said to myself, what a bad omen to have in my life.

When I came to this country in 1980, I was instantly attracted to light in complexion women, irrespective of their race, and I got along with them very well. One day I went to a party and a friend introduced me to one of his female friends. We dated for a few months, and then got married on October 1981. When we met, she owned a house and I lived in an apartment. We were planning to move in together when I found out the kind of lifestyle she liked to live. She liked to have threesome kind of sex, and sometimes, she invited couples to her house, and they swap their partners during orgy sex. I was not into that kind of lifestyle, so in 1982 we separated, but remained as friends and then divorced in 1984.

After my divorce, I dated, but not in any serious relationships, because of all the turmoil I was going through in my life at the time. In the early part of 1994, I went to a friend's house and she introduced me to her cousin who was staying with her. Her cousin was from my mother's hometown in Nigeria. However, she was not light in complexion, but I liked her a lot. She was tall and pretty, and the more I knew her, my feelings towards her developed. I fell in love with her and I wanted to marry her. When we met, she was married, but was going through a divorce.

I knew that we did not have many things in common, but I decided to help her with her situation. She liked to eat out a lot, and I do not. She argued a lot, I do not. She talks a lot, and I do not. She liked to party a lot, I do not. We had the same blood type, which meant that, if she was pregnant, we had to worry about having a Sickle cell anemia baby.

Recognizing all those facts, I loved her and I was committed in helping her, so that she would be independent, have a decent job and plan her career goals in life. So in September 1994, we got married. I did not know that she was that stubborn until we were married and moved in together, that was when her stubbornness manifested itself, and I could not stand it. I really loved her, but it seems as if I was risking my life been with her, because of her behavior and the reckless way she lived her life. There was a time I thought to myself, maybe her attitude and behavior was just to show her friends that she was not in love with me. She did not care if she was seen with another man or not.

Some of her Nigeria male friends who she thought were her best friends, told me to dump her and not to marry her, and they were the friends she trusted. But she did not know that they said some nasty things about her, behind her back. After a while, we separated, and we continued as friends after our separation. However, I loved her so much that I would do anything to help her. We remained married, until I recognized that she was able to take care of herself, live her life, and try to accomplish her goals. Then we officially divorced in 1998, remained as friends and kept in contact with each other. I love her.

After my divorce in 1998, my mother introduced me to a young woman from my village back home in Nigeria. My mother knew her through her parents, because they were friends to our family. She sent me her pictures, I liked her, and I communicated with her through the telephone. I sent her money every month, and sometimes sent money to her parents too.

I traveled to Nigeria in 1999, spent about six weeks in Nigeria, and tried to know her and her parents as I stayed with my parents. For the weeks that I stayed in Nigeria, we did not have any intimate moments. Sometimes I wanted to have sex with her, but any time I made such a suggestion, she always had an excuse not to have sex.

The day we went to their house and paid some dowries to her parents, her behavior was so awkward, that when I went home with my parents, I told my mother about it. After I gave her parents the dowry money, I also gave her some spending money. She told me that the money I gave her was not enough, so I gave her more money. However, that incident arose my curiosity, and I asked myself this question, did she really love me, or my money? During my visit, we never spent any intimate moments together. The last two weeks of my stay in Nigeria, we did not see each other, because she said that she had some school projects to complete, so she went back to her school in another state.

When I came back to the United States of America, I did everything required by the Immigration and Nationalization Service, to get her a visa to come to the United States of America for us to be married. When her visa was approved, I bought a two-way airline ticket for her. That was from Nigeria to Seattle and back to Nigeria. The reason was that, the ticket was cheaper that way.

The day I met her at the Seattle airport, we did not kiss or anything like that. Though I wanted to kiss her, but there was this kind of cold feelings about her, as if she was not happy being with me. If two people are really in love, and had not seen each other for more than one year, and now they are together, they would have spent the night making love and getting to know each other the more. In my case, it did not happen that way. She took some shower, ate and then went to bed. The following morning, I asked her if everything was okay with her, she said yes, but that she missed her family. I showed her where all the food items where, and told her to feel at home and cook whatever she wanted to eat. Then I left for work.

I know how to cook, and if someone prepare the kind of food that I do not like, or that was not cooked properly, I do not care if that person was my mother or my wife, I would not eat it. I had no appetite for the kind of food she cooked one day when I came home from work, so I ate something else.

One day after she took a shower, I asked her to have sex with me, she told me that she was on her period. So I backed off. I noticed that anytime she took a shower, she had a jar of oil that she rubbed all over her body from head to toe. When I asked her what kind of oil was that, and why she rubbed it all over her body, she told me that her native pastor gave it to her. I asked her what was the oil intended to do for her? She said that it was to overcome some of the voodoo spell moments she had sometimes.

She told me that when she was in Nigeria, that one of her uncles that was jealous of their family, put a curse on her, not to recognize some immediate members of her family, and would not recognize me as her husband, and that she would never be in love with the man she wanted to marry. She told me many stories about voodoo spell, native medicine and rituals.

I did not have a long distance telephone company at the time of her visit. I used calling cards with different companies to make long distance calls. Sometimes we would be eating or sleeping, and someone would call from Nigeria. When I asked her who the person that called was, she told me that it was her uncle's wife. This woman must have called my house more than hundred times within the three weeks that my so called wife came and stayed with me.

When I asked her why her uncle's wife called that often, she said that she called to check on her problem with the voodoo spell, and wanted to know if she was getting better. Sometimes she would ask me for some calling cards to make calls to Nigeria, and I gave her some cards.

I noticed that sometimes, when I came back from work and wanted to rest, that we argued a lot, and most of our discussions were about the voodoo spell she told me she had. Any time she took a shower, and rubbed some oil all over her body, we did not discuss having sex at all. Some of the discussions were on the voodoo spell, and I had lots of headache discussing that issue.

It happened that one day I went to work, and she wanted to call Nigeria and talk to some family members. Since I did not have long distance telephone Company, she called me at work and wanted to use one of my calling card numbers to call Nigeria. So I told her to wait on the phone while I use one of the numbers to place the call to Nigeria.

She was on hold while I connected the call. It was a three way connection, but once the call went through, I did not speak, and pretended as if I was off the phone. I use my hand to block the mouthpiece of the phone. The phone rang for a while, before I heard the voice of a man on the Nigeria end of the phone. So I listen to their conversation without her knowing that I was listening.

She told the man on the phone that everything was going according to plan, and that we were about to go to court and get married in the next few days, and then I would get her a green card that would allow her to stay and work in the United States of America. She told him that once she received the card, that she would divorce me and move to California, where she had some of her relatives. She said that she would then plan on how to bring him over to the United States of America, so that they would be married. During their conversations, that was when I knew that the man on the phone was her boyfriend.

She told the boyfriend that I had wanted to have sex with her, and that she told me that she was on her period, so that I would not have sex with her. She told him that she did not want to get pregnant and have any kids with me, and that was the reason she did not want to have sex with me in the first place. She also told him that the voodoo spell plan she was using as an excuse was working, because she had told me that she did not recognize me as her husband.

After she finished talking to her boyfriend, I almost fainted, but I kept my composure so that my coworkers would not know the kind of shock that I had. That same day she called me and wanted to talk to her sister in Nigeria, so I used another calling card and connected her to her sister. During their conversations, I discovered that her sister knew what she had planned. How she wanted to marry me just to get her green card, divorce me and then marries her boyfriend in Nigeria. Then, with the green card that she would get from me, she would use it to bring her boyfriend to the United States of America, so that both of them would live together.

Most of the times that we spent together, and I requested that we had sex, she gave me one excuse or another. One of the excuses, was that she was on her period. When she told her sister how she had used her period as an excuse not to have sex with me, the sister asked her how long she would use that excuse, since both of us lived together. She told the sister that she would use that excuse as long as she could, and that the voodoo spell plan was also working as an excuse. Her sister told her that it was not fair to treat me that way, because I had done a lot for her.

When I got home from work, I acted as if I did not know her plans, and that I did not hear what she said, when she made those phone calls to her boyfriend in Nigeria. I also noticed that she did not like to spend some time with me. We did not eat together, we did not curdle, kiss or have sex as much as I would have wanted. For the three weeks she lived with me, we only had sex once, and she made sure that I did no ejaculate in her.

If I was in the living room, she went to the bedroom, if I was in the bedroom, she stayed in the living room. Her uncle's wife called her mostly when I was at work. Therefore, she must have told her, that was the best time to call to prevent me from knowing what they discussed. During the period that she came to live with me, my mother visited us in the United States of America, and had surgery on her leg. She had urged me several times to get married, and finally, the woman she introduced me to marry was here for us to live together and be married.

If I told my mother, what the woman she wanted me to marry intended to do to me, she would think that I made up another excuse not to get married. I knew there was no way I would have convinced my mother, that the woman she wanted me to marry, had that kind of devious mind towards me. That she never intended to marry me in the first place. All she wanted to do, was to use me to bring her boyfriend over here, so that both of them could get married after she divorced me.

One day, when I got off work, I went to an electronic store on my way home, and bought some telephone recording gadgets. After I hooked up the telephone recording device to my phone, I showed her how to operate the different buttons in the recorder, and the button to push if she was on the phone and did not want her conversations to be recorded. The device had a red indicator light, that lit up if any conversation was recorded. She liked talking on the phone, and whenever the telephone rang, she answered it, before she gave it to me, if the person wanted to talk to me.

My intention for buying the telephone recording device, was to record her conversation through her mistake, if she did not push the do not record button during her conversations. I also wanted her to be the one that would tarnish her own reputation, and brought her own downfall, because of her conspiracy against me.

Any day I came home from work, I looked at the telephone recorder light, to see if any conversations was recorded. There was none, which meant that she knew how to use the recorder. One day I looked at the telephone recorder, and the indicator light was lit up, which meant that some conversations were recorded. May be she became accustomed to the telephone recorder, had a nonchalant attitude, and was reluctant to push the do not record button, and some of her conversations were recorded. I waited a few days before I replayed the conversations, and noticed that she was talking to her uncle's wife. In one of the conversations, she advised her to keep on using the voodoo spell, and her period not to have sex with me as excuses, since both were working.

Every day when I came home from work and wanted to rest, all our discussions were on the voodoo spell she said that was cast on her. I was so exhausted discussing the issue, that I said to myself, God, what I had gotten myself into. I prayed and asked God to give me a nice wife, and now this.

I told her that I did not know anything about voodoo spell, since my family was not involved in that kind of rituals. She kept asking me for suggestions, because she said that she was losing her mind, that the voodoo spell on her was getting worse, and that she did not love me, and did not want me to be her husband. I told her that since she said that she was getting worse, maybe she had to visit Nigeria for some treatment. I also told her that she had a return ticket, which she could use to go to Nigeria, since her visa was good for one year, and after her treatment, that I would buy her another flight ticket to come back to the United State of America.

When I made all those comments to her, all I had in mind was that if she ever went back to Nigeria, she would never come back to me again. The following day, after I got off work, I told my senior brother what had happened. How the woman I thought I was going to marry, had planned to use me to bring her Nigeria boyfriend over to the United States of America.

I told him all the things she told me about the voodoo spell she said that one of her uncles cast on her. I also told him everything I heard during her conversation with her boyfriend in Nigeria. I told my brother, how I planned to send her back to Nigeria with the return flight ticket I bought for her, and that I did not want our sister and mother to know about my plans, until she left Seattle Airport on her way to New York to meet my other brother.

I told my brother in New York about what happened, and the date I had planned that my so called wife would leave Seattle Airport to New York. I told him never to let her felt as if she was not coming back to the United Stated of America. To act as if he did not know what had happened, and to make her feel at home when she arrived in New York.

Before she travelled, I had already recorded some phone conversations that I would use as evident on how she wanted to use me to bring her boyfriend over to the United States of America. My mother was staying at my sister's house after her surgery. So my intention was that the day I would tell my mother, that the woman she wanted me to marry, planned to use me to bring her boyfriend over here, I would play the tape for her to hear exactly what she said on those tapes, and that would convince my mother that what I told her was the truth.

Whenever we talked about her voodoo spell problems, I acted, and told her that she would come back to the United States of America after her treatment. Two days before she departed for New York, we went shopping. I bought her some clothes, shoes, and many other items. I also bought some items for her family. I did not want her to talk on the phone anymore, because I did not know what kind of idea her uncle's wife would give her, if she knew she was coming back to Nigeria. Therefore, I took two days off from work, just to stay home and answer the phone calls.

Those two days I stayed at home with her was not enjoyable, because we did not do anything for fun. When I went to use the bathroom, I unplugged the phone, so that she did not get any calls. After she took her shower, she asked me if there was a problem with the telephone, because she did not get any calls for the day. I told her that the telephone was okay. She asked me if I had some calling cards, so that she would make some phone calls to Nigeria. I had some cards, but I purposely told her that I had none.

For the period of time she was with me, I made sure I kept her passport and the flight ticket with me. I did that, because on one of her calls to her boyfriend and her uncle's wife, she had told them that she might run away to San Francisco, where some of her relatives lived. So when she asked me where her passport and flight ticket was, I told her that I had used it to book her return flight to Nigeria. I also made sure that all the things she parked in her luggage, were all the stuff I wanted her to take, and not my personal belongs.

The day she travelled, I woke up and prepared the breakfast for both of us. A few hours before her departure, I noticed some hesitation, and that she did not want to travel any more, and she told me that maybe it was not a good idea to travel back to Nigeria. I reassured her that it was the best thing for her to do, and since her visa was good for one year, to visit the United States of America, that it would be better to go and receive some treatment, and then come back refreshed.

Her flight to New York was to leave around 7pm at night that day, but we left my apartment around 4pm, just to avoid any more telephone calls. I took her to some drive through restaurant, bought some foods, and we ate in the car while we cruised through the city of Seattle, and spent some time before we went to the airport.

We arrived at the airport around 5:30pm and she checked in her luggage. I waited until I made sure that she had boarded the plane, and it took off to New York. I got into my car and prayed, and thanked God for showing me the kind of woman she was before I committed myself to her. Because all those things happened within three weeks after she came to Seattle.

As she was on her way to New York, I phoned my sister and my mother, and told them what had happened. That the woman she wanted me to marry, was on her way to Nigeria via New York, and never to come back to Seattle. My sister was crying on the phone, and said that she did not believe what I just told them. I told her that I was on my way to her house with the recorded phone conversation tapes I had, so that I would play them for her and my mother to hear.

When they heard what was on the tapes, they were baffled that she had such a devious mind. On those taped conversations, her uncle's wife told her that as long as the voodoo spell plan was working, let her keep using it, and to make sure not to have sex with me, to avoid being pregnant. My mother and sister thanked God, that she demonstrated what kind of person she was, before we got married.

When she arrived at New York, my brother was waiting for her at the airport. She spent one day at my brother's house, and I was very grateful for the hospitality my brother and his family gave her, because they made her feel at home. Then the following day, she boarded the plane to Nigeria. Upon her arrival in Nigeria, she phoned and told me that she arrived safely, and that she was looking forward to coming back to the United States of America after her voodoo spell treatment.

I told her that there was no need for her to come back to the United States of America, because my engagement to her was over. I also told her that I would not buy her any flight ticket to come back to the United States of America, and that I did not want her to call me on the phone any more. I later phoned her parents, and told them that my engagement to their daughter was over, and that they could keep the dowry money I had already given them.

Her mother died a few months after I broke up my engagement to her daughter, and many people attributed her death to the broken heart, she had after I called off my engagement to her daughter, coupled with her illness. That was because during my engagement to her daughter, I sent money to them every month, but when I broke up the engagement, I stopped sending money to them. Afterwards. I found out that her Nigeria boyfriend dumped her and married someone else. About one year after the death of her mother, her sister died, and that was the last time I heard anything about that family.

Life after the nightmare of my wishful married life

After my dreadful experience with married life, the one question I kept asking myself was, am I destined not to get married, and have children of my own? I admire and adore pretty women, and I tend to pamper the women I fell in love with. I love kids, and I wish that I had them sooner in my lifetime, raise them in a Christian way of life, and then see them grow into adulthood. However, those things I loved and cherished in my life had eluded me to this day. I still hope that one day, by the grace of God, I will find the woman of my dreams to have a lasting relationship with, and then get married and have children, regardless of my age.

I recognized that this was not how I planned my life, because if all things were equal, and I did not encounter all those discriminations and injustices, I would have had a wife with grown up children by now. I would have had enough money to take care of myself, and the once that I loved and cared for, and help my fellow human beings. However, because of all the misfortunes and injustices I encountered in my life, I am still struggling to survive.

God, your time is the best. If you decide that I will have those things in my life before I die, I will have them. If the alternative is the case, I will assume, that is how I will leave my life, and I thank you for that. I knew that some people have doubts that I might not be able to get a woman pregnant, and that was the reason why I did not want to get married again.

The answer I gave to any of the people with those doubts, was for them to bring their sisters, wives, nieces, cousins and aunts to me, so that I would experiment by having sex with them, and then see if they could be pregnant or not. However, it should be under certain conditions. The women should not be fat, and most be pretty.

Finally, God, I am worn out with grief, and some nights, my pillow is soaked with tears, for this journey had been painful. But I had kept the promise I made to you. I would finish my memoir with this special prayer to my God.

Lord in your hands
I give my soul

God, you are all I want in this life, have mercy on me, and listen to my cry for help, for I am worn out with grief. Every day and night, my eyes are damped from my tears. My prayers go up to you, show me the way I should go, for you are my God. Teach me to do your will and protect me from all evils.

Lord, I cry to you for help, for I am sunk in despair. Hear my prayers, and set me free from my distress. Answer me God at a time you choose, for you are my Lord. Everything I have and cherished that you have given me, I surrender them all to be guided by your will. Your love and grace are wealth enough for me.

Teach me to realize that our stay in this world is short, and it is a staging place for the preparation and happiness of my true future, which is in heaven where life is external.

Oh Lord in your hands I give my soul. Father, I give my life to you. Do with me whatever you will, for you are my Lord. I am ready, and will accept whatever you decide to do with my life. I do hope that you will give me the strength, will power and blessing to overcome the grieves.

God make us all learn to live in peace, practice what is demanded by Justice, and respect the rights of every individual. Oh Lord my God, let me never think of evil to anyone. If I have wronged anyone, betrayed a friend, or without cause done violence to anyone, God please forgive me.

I thank you Lord for all you have done for me, and I ask that in my dying moment that you will forgive me of all my sins. Please help prepare me through the hours of my death, and then call me to stay with you. Grant this through Christ our Lord. Amen.

In conclusion, people should learn to forgive one another of their discretions. If we can commit all kinds of atrocities, and then ask for God's forgiveness, then we should forgive our fellow human being, when they do us some wrong. You might not forget the wrong done to you, but at least learn to forgive, so that you can start to rebuild your life again.

CPSIA information can be obtained at www.ICGtesting.com
Printed in the USA
LVOW06s0220110915

453780LV00018B/159/P